DOES THE BLACK MIDDLE CLASS EXIST AND ARE WE MEMBERS?

DOES THE BLACK MIDDLE CLASS EXIST AND ARE WE MEMBERS?

Reflections from a Research Team

BY

GRACE KHUNOU
University of the Witwatersrand, South Africa

KRIS MARSH
University of Maryland, USA

POLITE CHAUKE
University of the Witwatersrand, South Africa

LESEGO PLANK
University of Johannesburg, South Africa

LEO IGBANOI
National Institute for Legislative and Democratic Studies, Nigeria

MABONE KGOSIEMANG
University of Johannesburg, South Africa

United Kingdom – North America – Japan – India
Malaysia – China

Emerald Publishing Limited
Howard House, Wagon Lane, Bingley BD16 1WA, UK

First edition 2020

Copyright © 2020 Grace Khunou, Kris Marsh, Polite Chauke, Lesego Plank, Leo Igbanoi and Mabone Kgosiemang

Published under exclusive licence

Reprints and permissions service
Contact: permissions@emeraldinsight.com

No part of this book may be reproduced, stored in a retrieval system, transmitted in any form or by any means electronic, mechanical, photocopying, recording or otherwise without either the prior written permission of the publisher or a licence permitting restricted copying issued in the UK by The Copyright Licensing Agency and in the USA by The Copyright Clearance Center. No responsibility is accepted for the accuracy of information contained in the text, illustrations or advertisements. The opinions expressed in these chapters are not necessarily those of the Author or the publisher.

British Library Cataloguing in Publication Data
A catalogue record for this book is available from the British Library

ISBN: 978-1-83867-356-7 (Print)
ISBN: 978-1-83867-353-6 (Online)
ISBN: 978-1-83867-355-0 (Epub)

Printed and bound by CPI Group (UK) Ltd, Croydon, CR0 4YY

ISOQAR certified Management System, awarded to Emerald for adherence to Environmental standard ISO 14001:2004.

Certificate Number 1985
ISO 14001

INVESTOR IN PEOPLE

CONTENTS

About the Authors — vii
Acknowledgements — xiii
Preface: Implicating our Bodies in Researching The Black Middle Class — xvii

1. Who is the Black Middle Class in History and Theory? — 1
2. The Black Middle Class: A Conceptual Moving Target? — 35
3. Those Snobbish "Clever" Blacks: Preconceived Notions of the Black Middle Class — 65
4. Thank You, but I Got this: Gender Dynamics Between Researchers and the Black Middle Class — 85
5. What do I Wear, and do I Eat their Food? Performing Middle Classness — 113
6. Conclusion — 143

Bibliography — 149
Index — 165

ABOUT THE AUTHORS

Grace Khunou, PhD: Professor Grace Khunou was awarded her PhD from Wits in 2007, resulting from a PhD fellowship from the Wits Institute for Social and Economic Research. She is currently a Professor in the Sociology Department at the UJ. She is C-rated by the National Research Foundation. She was a senior lecturer at the School of Human and Community Development at Wits from 2010 to 2013 and served as the chairperson of the Wits Humanities Transformation Committee. She was the President of the South African Sociological Association (SASA) in 2015–2016, and the Vice-Dean of Research in the Humanities at UJ in 2015–2016. Professor Khunou has also served in the Council of SASA and was part of the editorial collective for the South African Sociological Review from 2012 to 2014. She is currently a member of the executive for the International Sociological Association and a member of the editorial board for the ISA SAGE in International Sociology. Her research is in understanding the Black condition through a focus on gender, health, social policy, class (the Black middle class) and social institutions. She writes creatively and academically and has published in peer-reviewed journals as well as book chapters and research reports. These include the collection *South Africa's Emergent Middle Class* (2015) and a special issue on father absence in the *Open Family Studies Journal* (2015), both of which she edited, and her recent co-edited book, Khunou, G. Phaswana,

E. Khosa-Shangase, K. & Canham, H. (2019). *Black Academics' Voices: The South African Experience* (2019). Her creative work includes the short story *Mama's Walk* in the 2012 Caine Prize for African Writers, and a children's book titled *Khumo's Airport Bag* (2015) published in Setswana and English. She is passionate about mentorship and has successfully supervised over 30 research projects. She has also presented more than 60 papers in international and local conferences.

Kris Marsh, PhD: Professor Kris Marsh received her PhD from the University of Southern California in 2005. She was a Postdoctoral Scholar at the Carolina Population Center at the University of North Carolina before joining the faculty of Maryland where she has been tenured since 2014. Professor Marsh's general areas of expertise are the Black middle class, demography, racial residential segregation and education. She has combined these interests to develop a research agenda that is divided into two broad areas: avenues into the Black middle class and consequences of being in the Black middle class. Currently, she is writing a book for Cambridge University Press on the wealth, health, residential choices and dating practices of members of an emerging Black middle class who are single and living alone. She also teaches courses on Research Methods, Race Relations and Racial Residential Segregation. She has been a visiting scholar at the University of Southern California, the University of the Witwatersrand in Johannesburg and the UJ. She has served as a contributor to CNN in America, the Associated Press, NBC Washington and Al Jazeera America and is frequently asked to contribute to the Washington Post. She serves as the secretary of the District of Columbia Sociological Society and the managing editor of *Issues in Race & Society*. She was awarded the Jacquelyn Johnson Jackson Early Career Award from the Association of Black Sociologists in 2015 and received the Core Fulbright U.S. Scholar award for 2017. While completing her Fulbright in South Africa, She was awarded the Excellence in Service Medal for Outstanding Faculty from the University of Maryland's Office of Multi-ethnic Student Education. Her most recent research and intellectual endeavours centre on improving police-community relations. Since late 2015, she has been the driving force behind a bias-free training and research collaboration between Prince George's County Police Department and the University of Maryland.

Leo Igbanoi, DLitt et Phil: Leo Igbanoi received his doctorate from the UJ in 2019 having been a recipient of the Global Excellence Stature Fellowship between 2016 and 2018. He was a lecturer in Gender Studies in the Department of Sociology at the UJ before joining the National Institute for Legislative and Democratic Studies, Abuja, where he is a Social Sector Analyst and teaches a course on Citizens and Political Change. He was a visiting research scholar at the University of Maryland in 2018. In 2010, he was awarded the Prize for African Studies at the Arrupe Jesuit University, Harare. His research interests include black masculinities, the black middle class, migration in Africa and the intersections of gender and social policy. He has presented papers at local and international conferences, and has been a contributor in two books, including *Treatise on Legislative Capacity Development for Good Governance in Nigeria* (2019).

Lesego Plank: Lesego Plank was awarded her Masters in Sociology from the University of Johannesburg in 2018 for a study titled *The Experiences of Single Black Middle Class Women from Soweto of Intimate Relationships*. She is currently a PhD candidate at UJ, under the Department of Sociology. Her PhD is focusing on Black motherhood, particularly the aspect of absent mothers and the idea of how motherhood in Black families is not biological. She is also a member in good standing of the UJ Post Graduate Association (PGA) in which she serves the PGA office as an academic officer. She has worked as an undergraduate tutor at the Department of Sociology (2015–2016), is currently working as a research assistant supervised by Professor Grace Khunou and has worked in various other projects as a research assistant. She has also worked as a project consultant for the company Quest Research Services. She has attended and presented her work at SASA and other forums on the black middle class and fatherhood. In 2017, she attended and participated in the Decolonial Black Feminism School held in Cachoeira, Bahía (Brazil). In 2018, she was a visiting emerging scholar at the University of Maryland in the US. Her research interests are in the Black middle class, Black motherhood, the African Black family and gender studies.

Mabone Kgosiemang: Mabone Kgosiemang is currently a PhD candidate in Sociology. He has obtained all his academic qualifications from the UJ. He was active in student politics in his undergraduate and early post-graduate years. He worked as a tutor in the Department of Sociology in 2016 and 2017. In 2018, he was appointed an assistant lecturer in the Department of Sociology at UJ. He has taught on Religion and Deviance, Power, State and Workplace and finally Social Inequality, focusing on Race, Class and Gender. He is a SASA member, a former SASA council member and has presented and chaired multiple times at SASA conferences. His recent publication is titled "*University Transformation Re-imagined: Discourses Resulting After the Fallist Movements*" (2018) in the book *We Are No Longer at Ease: The Struggle for #FeesMustFall*. Johannesburg: Jacana. His research interests are on race and racism, student politics, higher education, transformation and decolonisation.

Polite Chauke: Polite Chauke is a PhD candidate and a teaching assistant at the University of the Witwatersrand in the Social Work Department. She is also a research member of the School of Human and Community Development (SHCD) research cluster team called WITSIE (Women Intellectuals Transforming Scholarship In Education) which focuses on the research on Sexual and Reproductive Health Rights, Gender Based Violence and Sexual Harassment in Higher Learning Institutions. Her publications include the article, *"Shaming Fathers into Providers: Child Support and Fatherhood in the South African Media"* (2015); *"Half of the picture: Interrogating common sense gendered beliefs surrounding sexual harassment practice within higher education"* (2015) and *"The grenade, the murder and the truth: The TRC's Section 29 inquiry for Rownan Fernandes"* (2016). Her research interests are in gender, fatherhood and sexual and reproductive health rights (SRHR) and her PhD focus are on cancer and the narratives of black women.

ACKNOWLEDGEMENTS

There are several people who made this project possible. We begin by thanking the beautiful people of South Africa. They allowed us to interview them for our study on the Black middle class. We appreciate the support from our University of Johannesburg (UJ), University of Maryland and University of Witwatersrand for helping to make this project possible. Many colleagues and associates helped to bring this book to fruition, and we thank each and every one of them with the deepest and most heartfelt appreciation possible.

We would each like to personally thank our friends and family members.

Grace Khunou: I am thankful for the great spirit of resistance shown continually and without fail by my people over the centuries – *Thokozani Bo Gogo*. May we continue to drink from your overflowing love. For this project, I am grateful to the UJ International Office and Research Office for their financial support, to the National Research Foundation grant for rated researchers and to my department for providing space for me to do this work. I am also grateful for the writing space provided by Johannesburg Institute for Advanced Study during this project. To my extended family and friends, your counsel and love keep me fearless. To everyone who gave of their time during the study, we are forever indebted to you – *Namaste*.

Kris Marsh: I begin with the acknowledgement that "I can do all things through Jesus Christ, that strengthens me" (Philippians 4:13). Thank you to my family for their never-ending support. To my close friends for calling, texting, emailing and writing to me when I was in South Africa and while I completed this project. Words simply cannot express the gratitude I feel for every prayer you prayed, every word of encouragement you uttered, and every ounce of love you showed me through this entire process. I appreciate you beyond words. I would be more than remiss if I did not mention several organizations that offered support one way or another during this journey: the Dean's Research Initiative Seed Grant, University of Maryland; University of Maryland, Office of International Affairs, Global Partnerships-Faculty Travel Grant; and the Fulbright U.S. Scholar Program for a grant for research in South Africa, 2017. The Fulbright experience allowed me to meet the wonderful people of South Africa and forever changed my life in so many positive ways.

Polite Chauke: To Professor Kris Marsh, thank you for opening yourself to South Africa, thank you for hearing our hearts, for that is where our stories lie. Thank you for this opportunity as it led us to your home and the world. May God bless everything you touch. Professor Grace Khunou, thank you for loving us, for making us a part of your success. You are a living ancestor who keeps paving new histories that make it possible for girls like me to exist. Thank you for being a constant disruption who seeks to make us great; you make me great. You make God smile and your ancestors dance – may they all bless you endlessly.

To my mother, father, my sisters and the Chauke family; thank you for choosing me every day and loving me stubbornly and shirtlessly. You are my lifeline, forever and always. To all the participants, thank you for stories and humanity – may

God bless you all. To the research team, it was amazing to have worked beside great minds, you are the beautiful ones Africa's been waiting for – bless up to each of you.

Lesego Plank: To my family *abakwa* Plank and the Nyanisa's, thank you for your constant support and love. To Professor Grace Khunou and Professor Kris Marsh, thank you for entrusting me to be part of this study and making a contribution in so many ways. I have learnt a lot from this project academically, personally and spiritually and I have gained a lot from this journey. To the participants I interviewed, your experiences and your thoughts, the conversations we had, have really encouraged me to be and do better. Thank you. To my friends, thank you for being there and for being proud of me. Thank you for the constant video calls and phones calls to check up on me when I was in America. To the whole research team, thank you, beautiful souls. You are a force to be reckoned with in the academic space! Remember Black child, we are our ancestor's wildest dreams!

Leo Igbanoi: Loving thanks to Atinzwaishe for being a constant pillar of strength to me, and for caring for the boys when I was far away from home during this research. Special appreciation to my family members and friends who, through constant calls and messages, followed my progress during this project, in both South Africa and the USA. Makari, you are forever cherished; thank you for being a true friend. I am indebted to you, Kris, for welcoming me into your beautiful home in Maryland; we made good memories even as we spent time writing. Thank you to the International Office at the UJ for a travel grant awarded to me for this project, and the research award from the University of Maryland to spend some time in the USA. Finally, my deepest appreciation goes to God who continues to lead me to where His grace sustains me.

Mabone Kgosiemang: I would like to thank and acknowledge everyone who has supported my academic growth and development, especially Professor Grace for being there during the entire journey. To my friends, both Magents and those from the academy: thank you for pushing me on days I felt tired and demotivated. To Professor Grace and Professor Kris thank you for the opportunity, in both South Africa and the United States; I grew and learned a lot. UJ and the Department of Sociology there, I thank you for the intellectual advancement; may other young Black academics experience similar. To my family, the Kgosiemang family, who my ancestors gave me and God blessed me with, I thank, love and appreciate you. None of this would be possible without your love, peace and belief in me. To my ancestors and God, may my prayers continue to be heard.

If we forgot to mention you, please charge it to our heads and not to our hearts!

PREFACE: IMPLICATING OUR BODIES IN RESEARCHING THE BLACK MIDDLE CLASS

Blackness is as open and as complex as the wide turbulent seas. This openness is a challenge and opportunity for those of us who work in black studies to trace and unfurl the contours and untangle the knots of the multiple ways of being black in the world. The black middle class is one of the strands of blackness that the academy has taken a keen interest in. This curiosity has been driven by multiple agendas which span from narrow consumerism which sees black people as not just workers but as eaters with increasingly refined and expensive tastes. This research has been about critically engaging with processes that cultivate a capitalist market for growing profits in an increasingly unequal world. At the other end of the spectrum are researchers committed to the nuances in identity that have emerged as a consequence of class transitions. Here, there is an increased concern with the ethics of class and self-reflexivity on the part of those doing this research. This book falls within the latter category of work. Grace Khunou has been on the edge of the black middle class wave of research over the past decade. Ever ahead of the wave, in this collection she is joined by African American scholar Kris Marsh and together they turn around to think about the process and meanings associated with researching the black middle class. But they take it a step further to think together with students for a communal reflection of what it means to do this research. This is a crucial turn because it centres reflections of graduate students in the cusp of their own class transition. In South Africa and elsewhere, it is still fair to say that the more education one has, the greater the likelihood they have to enter into a new class position if they and their families had previously been working class as has been the case for the majority of black South Africans. But class movement is complex and does not occur in a straight line. These reflections point to these movements and the nuances in the lives of the researchers.

Class scholarship in South Africa has long needed a truly intersectional lens. The strength of this work is the positionality of the contributors. They are mostly women, they are black, and they inhabit class jauntily as largely first generation black middle class persons or in the liminal spaces between classes. Their reflections about their work on this topic are inflected with their own positioning and negotiations of intersecting identities. In this volume, we have the opportunity to see novice scholars cut their teeth in the academy under the sisterly guidance of experienced editors. This is not a trite undertaking. It as an important political intervention for both class scholarship and mentorship of the next generation of researchers. Khunou and Marsh do not just bemoan the marginalization of black women in the South African and global academy – they intervene decisively. This project bears witness to this. I frame this intervention as decolonial because decolonization is a process of doing. It not only challenges coloniality but leads to discernible change.

Our scholarship is better for this intervention. We now have a perspective of what it means to do this research in an ethical and embodied way from black peoples varying positionalities. With the publication of this volume, we no longer have to rely only on 'objective' accounts that do not implicate the bodies of those who produce scholarship about others.

Hugo Canham, Associate Professor of Psychology,
University of the Witwatersrand

1

WHO IS THE BLACK MIDDLE CLASS IN HISTORY AND THEORY?

INTRODUCTION

Since the African Development Bank published *The Middle of the Pyramid: Dynamics of the Middle Class* in 2011, studies on the Black middle class in South Africa have proliferated. These studies have confirmed that the Black middle class is on the rise (Khunou, 2015a; Krige, 2012; Ndletyana, 2014; Southall, 2016; Statistics South Africa, 2009). The growth of a Black middle class has been regarded as an important benchmark for Blacks' social, political and economic standing. Ndletyana (2014) suggests that middle classes are also important for strengthening democracies, as their power lies mostly in their citizenship rights.

We will see, however, that the definition of middle class is a shifting target. While many studies grapple with how to define the Black middle class, and some try to unpack self-definitions of middle class, this study, unusually, turns the lens on the researchers as well as the researched in order to get a handle on a slippery concept. As Black researchers studying the Black middle class, we recognised the importance of reading ourselves as possible insiders and outsiders to the middle class position and how that impacted how we engaged with the participants and theorising on the concept. In our endeavours to do research, we have engaged emerging researchers in this project as important knowledge creators and not as merely fieldworkers as is done in most studies.

This chapter will outline some of the challenges of defining the concept through a historical and theoretical lens before introducing reflexivity as a tool to better meet these challenges.

The social mobility of Blacks into the middle class position is often purported to be evidence that racial discrimination and prejudice have eroded; this is assumed even when continuing inequalities illustrate the continuities of discrimination. In South Africa, this growth is also erroneously viewed as an indicator of a shift from the significance of race to the importance of class as an analytical lens. Seekings (2013) suggests that at some point during apartheid and in post-apartheid South Africa, the privileges enjoyed by Whites became more about their class position rather than a result of racial discrimination. The analytical lens provided by Seekings (2013) is skewed as there is an underlying suggestion that, when not legislated, racial discrimination disappears. Such a lens fails to acknowledge the enduring link between racialisation and resource allocation (Posel, 2010). Again, the privileges accrued as a result of racial discrimination are maintained in multiple ways including continued racial discrimination (Canham, 2014) with regards to access to jobs, and the continued racially skewed access to the economy. This continued link between race and resources remains, but it is important to acknowledge that the growth of the Black middle class since 1994 is a result of the democratic state's attempts at racial redress (Ndletyana, 2014).

The fact that the Black middle class makes up two-thirds of the South African middle class is a key factor in the misconception that class has become more significant since 1994 (Canham & Williams, 2017). Similarly, Krige (2012) shows that the size of the Black middle class remains significantly low in South Africa. Additionally, Mattes (2014) warns that the emergence of the Black middle class does not necessarily equate to political difference within societies. For instance, in post-apartheid South Africa, most townships and rural areas, which are predominantly Black, are still struggling to access basic necessities such as water, sanitation and electricity, and in other township areas they still live in overcrowded backyard shacks (Beall, Crankshaw, & Parnell, 2002; Mattes, 2014). This indicates how the notion of "middle class" in South Africa is complex, context-dependent and thus regarded as problematic. One of the major reasons for this is the historical basis of colonisation and apartheid, as these systems produced high levels of inequality in the country (Khunou, 2015a).

The middle class position has different elements to it; it would thus be erroneous to assume it is a homogenous group. Research shows that the middle class is made up of different categories, such as lower, middle and upper middle class categories (Burger, McAravey, & Van der Berg, 2015; Visagie, 2013). Scholars such as Bourdieu (1996) and Fulton, Furman, and Findlay (2014) have argued that those who are in the upper middle class position are perceived as being more affluent than those in the middle and lower middle class categories; they have the ability to choose and they are afforded the choice to spend and are able to save more money compared to other middle class categories. For example, Southall (2013) shows how, in South Africa, the annual income in the year 2000 for those in the upper middle class was more than Rs. 150,000, and for those in the lower middle class position it was around Rs. 59,000 in a year. The upper middle class are believed to be working as highly qualified specialists, who are highly educated and are occupying high level managerial positions compared to those who are lower middle class, who work as clerks, lower level managers, sales persons, middle managers and crafts people (Fulton et al., 2014; Southall, 2013, 2016).

A HISTORICAL OVERVIEW OF THE BLACK MIDDLE CLASS

A historical analysis of South African society illustrates that the Black middle class is not a new phenomenon (Mabandla, 2013; Melber, 2017; Ndletyana, 2014; Southall, 2016). In historical studies, this category encompassed the notions of a well-established Black middle class that owned land and livestock (Bundy, 1988; Murray, 1992; Peires, 1989). The African middle classes were achieved mainly as a result of missionary stations during the colonialisation era (Mabandla, 2013; Ndletyana, 2014). The aim of Christian missionaries was to civilise the way of life of the Africans, believing that it did not fit in with their own colonial mandate and principles. The promotion of education, the demolition of traditional rondavel houses and their replacement with square houses, and the purchase of westernised furniture for their households, were ways of changing the way of life of Africans (Mabandla, 2013; Southall, 2016). The consumerist lifestyle of the African elite benefited the colonisers and capitalism in many ways.

Part of the civilising mission was to create a buffer class, a trend famous in the British divide and rule strategy (Ndletyana, 2014). This buffer class was created mainly through education and was also achieved by encouraging Africans to learn how to read the bible, as it was believed that this would make them repent of their evil ways of life and refrain from their traditional practices (Mabandla 2013; Melber, 2017).

Education of Africans meant that they could work as nurses, clerical officers, priests, farmers and teachers (Mabandla, 2013; Ndletyana, 2014). This afforded them the opportunity of being leaders in their community, because of their education status; they were able to speak the colonisers' language, write and understand most aspects of the colonisers and this advantage allowed them to represent their people (Southall, 2016). Despite their privilege over those who were poor and less educated, the Black middle class were still restricted in many ways by the colonial system. Melber (2017) contends that the major reason for their restriction and limitations was because of their race, and this meant that race for the African was a hindrance to their upward mobility. Likewise, during apartheid, class positions in the country were constituted on the basis of race – remember that apartheid was a system which prescribed racial segregation and discrimination for the benefit of the Whites (Khunou, 2015a). On the one hand, the system ensured that Whites were empowered, through ownership of the means of production, access to quality education, adequate housing and healthcare services (Melber, 2017). This was regarded as an act to actively build the White middle class and ensure its sustainability for years to come, thus even in contemporary South Africa, the White middle class is maintained. On the other hand, Blacks during apartheid were at the receiving end of disenfranchisement achieved through dispossession of land and subjugation (Ndletyana, 2014). Thus, Blacks in the middle class remained in the margins, with no equal access to opportunities like those that privileged and aided their White counterparts (Southall, 2013; Visagie, 2011).

Alternatively, scholars such as Hoosen and Mafukdze (2007), Ndletyana (2014) and Ngoma (2015) argue that, in many ways, the apartheid government endorsed the Black middle class as one of their strategic plans, as they wanted to create a division amongst Black people, creating a conflicting debate around "us" and "them" among Blacks. This was because in South Africa, there were very poor Blacks, who were even struggling to make ends meet, while the Black middle class were in a seemingly comfortable position, as they had access to a number of opportunities and lived a better life than poor or working class Blacks (Ngoma, 2015). For instance, most of the Black middle class lived in bigger and adequate houses, they were educated and had better job prospects and better income. The apartheid government was more invested in protecting their power and thus supported the Black middle class in order to create conflict, so that Black people become fragmented and do not focus on pertinent issues of the struggle against apartheid. During apartheid, some people who were middle class were regarded as sell-outs of the struggle as they were seen as allies of the apartheid government (Southall, 2016).

However, it is crucial to highlight that, even though the Black middle class were receiving benefits from the apartheid government, they were restricted in several ways and because of their race (Khunou, 2015a). In most cases, the Black middle class were mostly restricted to live in areas designated "Black". For example, Diepkloof extension was built for the Black middle class in the township of Soweto. They did not live in residential areas which were occupied by and reserved for Whites. This is an indicator of how the apartheid government promoted separatist development policies even amongst the middle class (Kros, 2010); thus, class was less significant as a marker of status and access for Blacks (Khunou, 2015a). Even when it came to employment opportunities, Black middle class professionals, such as nurses, teachers, police and social workers, were to work in the townships and treat other Black people, while White professionals were employed in predominately White areas and hardly worked in Black townships (Kros, 2010), which meant differential pay. Ngoma (2015) confirms that there were disparities in how they were paid: White middle class professionals were paid more than Black middle class professionals. Additionally, the working conditions for the Black middle class were inadequate (Kros, 2010): in hospitals, they had shortages of medication and resource limitations in public schools, where they had to deal with overcrowded classrooms, which made teaching difficult. These difficulties, writes Ndletyana (2014, p. 7), were because homelands – and one could say later townships – "were economically unviable and depended wholly on the apartheid government for their budgets".[1]

DEFINING THE BLACK MIDDLE CLASS

Defining "middle class" regardless of race has proven difficult (Alexander, Ceruti, Motseke, Phadi, & Wale, 2013; Southall, 2016; Visagie, 2013). This conceptual complexity is especially challenging when defining it with regards to Blacks because it has long been acknowledged that there exist oppressive, discriminatory and racist systems against Blacks in both South Africa and globally. Traditionally, social scientists have relied upon education, occupation, income, wealth and spending patterns as objective indicators of socio-economic well-being and middle class status (Babu, 2015; Ndletyana, 2014). Later studies on the Black middle class focused on urban populations and centred their conception of the Black middle class through the lens of income and occupation, with an emphasis on managerial and professional categories (Crankshaw, 1997; Rivero, Du Toit, & Kotze, 2003; Seekings & Nattrass, 2006). After 1994, popular conceptions of Black middle classness centre income, occupation and education (Visagie, 2013). Regardless of the measure used, they are not void of challenges.

The main challenge associated with using these traditional indicators of socio-economic and class status to define the Black middle class arises when scholars seek to make cross-racial, cross-national and global comparisons. From a racial perspective, this becomes problematic because of the large racial disparities in education, income, occupation and wealth that exist between Blacks and Whites (Burger et al., 2015; Carter, 2005; Collins, 1997; Darity & Mason, 2004; Zoch, 2015). From a national and international perspective, the challenge is when trying to compare the historical and contextual differences of these traditional measures.

When looking more closely at traditional measures of class, there are substantive limitations to such measures. Studies that focused on education have typically specified, at least, a bachelor's degree (Posel, 2010; Southall, 2016). In terms of income, researchers have relied upon an income range as well as median household income to determine middle class status (Burger, Steenekamp, Van der Berg, & Zoch, 2014). Income definitions meet with the most contestation, as some tend to lump lower classes with the middle class. For example, Ndletyana (2014) contends that income definitions lack nuance as they fail to include education and middle class lifestyles. Middle class occupations have been assessed based on blue-collar versus white-collar professions (Crankshaw, 1997; Landry, 1987; Rivero et al., 2003; Seekings & Nattrass, 2006; Wilson, 1978). Racial wealth disparities have a stubborn and persistent stronghold on South Africa, with Whites holding most of the wealth. It is clear from the social science literature that education, income and wealth are imperfect measures because large inequities exist among middle class Blacks and Whites. Despite the problematic nature of these objective measures, social scientists have used, and continue to use these same indicators to define the Black middle class (Southall, 2016).

More recently, Black middle class scholarship has extended research beyond utilising these traditional measures of socioeconomic status, and considered other dimensions such as neighbourhood location (Crankshaw, 2008; Krige, 2012); social class identification (Alexander et al., 2013); and the use of both objective and subjective measures (Alexander et al., 2013; Phadi & Ceruti, 2011). Yet even these subjective variables are problematic in nature.

For example, we consider more closely the challenges of the subjective measure of neighbourhood location. Middle class Blacks tend to live in less socioeconomically desirable neighbourhoods (Besteman, 2008; Lemanski, 2006; Pattillo-McCoy, 2013; Seekings, 2010). This is visible in South Africa where residential desegregation is a new phenomenon. With this desegregation comes an increase in Black home ownership, in which some would be moving from "apartheid defined residential spaces" and would move to areas, which are regarded as higher-income suburbs, which are still dominated by Whites (Krige, 2012).

On another note, there has been an increase in the renovation of pre-owned municipal houses in the townships by the Black middle class. The renovation of municipal houses and moves to the suburbs by the Black middle class have both been negatively viewed as conspicuous consumption, and thus the Black middle class have been viewed as wasting money (Krige, 2015).

The notion that the Black middle class are conspicuous consumers is based on a narrow conception of this group and a continuation of historical constructions of Blackness as lacking (Posel, 2010). Furthermore, there are negative social perceptions placed on Black wealth accumulation and expenditure, which their white counterparts do not have to contend with (Canham & Williams, 2017). The Black middle class in South Africa must struggle with negative stereotypes that limit Blackness to working class realities. Therefore, when the Black middle class have access to better housing, wealth, cars and luxuries that are often out of reach for the homogenised construction of South African Blackness, it is assumed they are living beyond their means, are in debt and it is simply defined as conspicuous consumption (de Coninck, 2018; Krige, 2012). These comments on the Black middle class as conspicuous consumers constitute continued racialisation of Blacks, because consumption by the White middle class in South Africa is normalised and not open to similar scrutiny, thus confirming Posel's (2010) assertion that consumption during apartheid was a racialising project meant to create whiteness.

Another challenge is that, regardless of racial disparities, Blacks have been increasingly more likely to self-identify as middle class, with education and income mainly influencing their identifications (Hunt & Ray, 2012; Krige, 2012). Self-identification with the middle or lower classes is influenced by the racial history of the country and the historical resource allocation, thus individuals position themselves in a relational context. They might position themselves lower or higher as compared to those they identify with (Alexander et al., 2013; Burger et al., 2014; Phadi and Manda, 2010).

Self-identification, although not a perfect measure, allows us to continue problematising simple conceptions of what it means to be middle class. On a similar note, Phadi and Ceruti (2011) also show the different contestations of defining the Black middle class, these scholars argue that people put different meanings to the term and that this depends on a number of factors, such as language, context, positionality and experience. For instance, in the study *Class in Soweto* (Alexander et al., 2013), a participant identified herself and her family as middle class, even though they lived in an informal settlement (Phadi & Ceruti, 2011). For this woman, they were middle class because they were not poor and they were not rich, they were in the middle, as they ate every day, had a shelter and had a generator, which their neighbours in the informal settlement did not have. This therefore indicates how the definition of the Black middle class is relative and difficult to conceptualise (Phadi & Ceruti, 2011; Visagie, 2013). Even though this self-identification as middle class is growing for Blacks, it is not without question. For example, Burger et al. (2014, p. 11) argue that there is a divergence between objective and subjective social class, thus refuting the assumption that there is an alignment between the two.

According to Burger (2014), there is discomfort and reluctance for some middle class Blacks to identify themselves as such. Khunou (2015a) illustrates how, because of the negative connotations linking the Black middle class to conspicuous consumption, some Black middle class people contest the meaning of the term and thus their self-identification with it. Spronk (2016) also indicates that self-identification with the term shifts in relation to where individuals find themselves in relation to others self-classified the same and classified by researchers and marketers the same. Again, the variety in the terms for self-identification with Black middle classness contributes to the contestations in conceptions of the term. For some of these reasons, scholars consider other subjective characteristics such as lifestyles and values, which hold significant meaning for the Black middle class (Frazier, 1957; Krige, 2012; Ndinga-Kanga, 2019; Pattillo-McCoy, 2013; Spronk, 2016; Lacy, 2007).

Regardless of the measurement used, much of the research in social sciences asserts that the middle class position achieved by Blacks is precarious (Khunou, 2015b; Southall, 2016), and thus demands scholarship that recognises the importance of "flexibility and instability over one's life course and even across generations" (Spronk, 2016, p. 12). Yet most scholars have neglected to allow the Black middle class to tell their story of what it means to be Black and middle class, largely because social science scholarship is still entrapped within the global power matrix and its colonial determinations. Scholars tend to overlook the agency in self-description and performances of middle class, maybe as a result of being "materialists" or "scientific" in their approach since, as Marx (1984) argues, "it is not the consciousness of men that determines their being, but rather their being which determines their consciousness", and thus they miss the diversity of conceptualisation that exists within the contested category "the Black middle class" (de Coninck, 2018). The large and persistent inequities between the Black and White middle classes, as well as scholarly disagreement over the definition of class, lead some to question the very existence of, and/or assume the fragility of, a Black middle class in South Africa and globally.

PRECONCEIVED NOTIONS IN SOCIAL RESEARCH: WHY REFLEXIVITY MATTERS

Reflexivity requires us to question our methods and allows us as researchers to take responsibility for our positionality and contribution to the research process. The building blocks of reflexivity are to pay particular attention to how our interests, beliefs and past experiences influence how we engage in research (Hesse-Biber & Leavy, 2011; King & Horrocks, 2010). As a result of taking up reflexivity as a method and stance the researcher remains constantly aware that they are an instrument that has opinions and experiences which may impact the research process and findings.

To avoid a lack of self-awareness, reflexivity provides the researcher with tools to show and explain methodological choices, changes and provide background information on their knowledge positions and theorisation. Self-awareness was central for us as Black researchers who through reflexivity were also in a way inserting ourselves in the study as knowledge creators (Khunou, Phaswana, Khosa-Shangase, & Canham, 2019). Berger (2015, p. 220) argues that reflexivity, "means turning of the researcher lens back onto oneself to recognise and take responsibility for one's own situatedness within the research and the effect that it may have on the setting and people being studied, questions being asked, data being collected and its interpretation". Therefore, in some cases, scholars such as Reid, Brown, Smith, Cope, and Jamieson (2018) suggest that interviewers and interviewees would mirror each other along dimensions and identities, such as socio-economic status, race, gender and language. Given the specific interest of this project, we grapple mainly with our own class status during interviews and how it influenced the interview process. However, given that class does not exist in a vacuum, we also address how gender influenced our encounter with the participants and their interaction with us. The interview process is dynamic and complex, and the gender, race, sexuality, age, class position and marital status of the researcher affect the research context and the type of knowledge developed (Khunou, n.d; Oakley, 1981). We are therefore of the opinion that sharing the usually undocumented personal experiences of the research process could improve our understanding of the research enterprise and therefore our data.

Research reflexivity is even more significant for studies on the Black middle class as it is a contested concept

(Khunou, 2015c; Phadi, 2010). This contestation is true even though the Black middle class has grown substantially since 1994 in South Africa. Given this contestation, and the dynamics that class inequality leads to, it is important to engage in reflexivity in interviewing the Black middle class and how a non-member vis-à-vis an internal member of that class group influences the interview process. Reflexivity becomes even more important in contemporary South Africa with the recent calls to decolonise knowledge and thus research methodologies. Doing reflexive work at this time in South Africa allowed us to raise important questions on how the insider/outsider dynamic is important to consider in how we think about what we know (Khunou et al., 2019) and what we do not know about our research participants. For example, Naples (1996, p. 84) cautions that "'Outsiderness' and 'Insiderness' are not fixed or static positions, rather they are ever-shifting and permeable social locations that are differentially experienced and expressed."

Researchers tend to experience research as both insiders and outsiders. Being an insider, as part of the research community in some form, allows for detailed data. Whereas, as an outsider, there is space for new observations, experiences and ideas about social phenomena. However, decolonial scholars caution against the dehumanising tendencies of researchers who consider themselves as only outsiders and thus objective. The human experience always makes us both. Therefore, for us it was important to grapple with the insider–outsider dichotomy through providing our "personal voices/narratives and subjective standpoints in the process of decolonizing monolithic dominant academic writing" (Gill, Pulu, & Lin, 2012, p. 2).

Furthermore, in understanding the insider–outsider dichotomy, researchers often find themselves switching between the two and need to reflect on how it influences their roles as writers and interviewers (Maxwell, Abrams, Zungu, & Mosavel, 2016; Simbürger, 2014). This dynamic was quite salient in our engagement with the study participants and is captured in our reflective process. We found resonance with Moore (2015) in that even though we considered ourselves outsiders with regards to some aspects of our participants, we were insiders with regards to others. It is also common for researchers to have preconceived ideas about the people they are studying. Researchers bring their experiences, knowledge, biases and selves as humans into qualitative research and this often calls for self-monitoring and critical reflection (Berger, 2015, p. 220). Even though this presents some challenges that researchers have been grappling with since the introduction of critical research methods and reflexivity, it has not been written about as often as it should be.

Fusch and Ness (2015, p. 1,411) argue that "researcher's bias/worldview is present in all social research, both intentionally and unintentionally". Researchers have particular positionalities, ideas and experiences; these influence how the researcher sees social research generally and their study participants in particular. This is why reflexivity is important. In a decolonial method, the intentions of reflexivity are also to humanise the research participants and to challenge our writing and theorising to include the human element (Gill et al., 2012). Also, the notions and subjectivities that researchers have can be a bias; this is why critical reflection allows for a process of remembering that researchers are part of the research process in a qualitative study (Berger, 2015; Finlay, 2002). In our engagement we were, therefore, conscious of Simbürger's (2014) warning that researchers need to think carefully about their bias as an interviewer and a writer. These dynamic processes bring different challenges, based on the human element in the interview process and, furthermore, on how ideology and subjectivities influence the writing process. Our reflexive process like in Khunou et al. (2019, p. 6) was an attempt at reimagining "knowledge, the knower, and knowing" and most importantly for us it was to reimagine the knowledge production process.

In our reflective discussion of the research process it was expected that the team held some preconceived ideas about the social phenomenon under investigation and about the participants. However, it is not easy to engage openly with one's preconceptions, especially when they are negative. This is one of the reasons why researchers might not be open to reflexivity (Finlay, 2002). What inspired us to write about our reflexivity in this book is a result of the recognition that, when not engaged with, such assumptions might impact the study negatively and paint the participants disparagingly, a notion that decolonial theorists advice against (Gill et al., 2012; Smith, 2008).

Again, what was important for us was how our different personal experiences, socio-economic backgrounds, international and national origins, ideological views and gender positions influenced how we viewed our participants. Additionally, the environments and social spaces in which research is conducted influence researchers and their views. Therefore, it remains critical to be reflexive so as to understand and review the insider–outsider contestation (Maxwell et al., 2016). It will be clear in the forthcoming chapters that because of our different yet fluctuating insider and outsider positionalities, we held different but fluid views of the research participants. Our experiences echo the argument made by Naples (1996) that insiderness and outsiderness are not fixed positions, and that a critical analysis of how the two manifest helps us understand the processes, which create otherness. Most importantly, it has allowed us to reimagine the knowledge production process.

GENDER DYNAMICS AND THE BLACK MIDDLE CLASS

As illustrated earlier, studies on the Black middle class have been on the increase since 1994. What is evident in most of the South African scholarship on the Black middle class is the paucity of a gender analysis. For example in many of these studies, including Alexander et al. (2013) and Phadi and Ceruti (2011), the multiple meanings of class position, issues of affordability, unemployment and social location are detailed without providing a gender analysis of those experiences. Feminist scholars clearly indicate how experiences of the world are gendered and further show that gender as an experience is located within cultural systems and therefore its history and articulations must be critically charted along with other aspects of social systems (Oyewumi, 1997, p. 79). It is therefore a serious limitation to engage in class analysis and research reflexivity without providing a gender lens.

Fieldwork in research is very crucial because this is where the researcher scrutinises the life of the participants. In research, gender has an influence on the research process, as gender dynamics affect the research project. Järviluoma, Moisala, and Vilkko (2011) argue that the concept of gender norms, its values, and the manner in which preconceptions arise when people of different genders or the same gender meet and how they interact with each other, is believed to be having a valued impact on the micro and macro levels of people's lives. These scholars further advise that in research, gender should be taken seriously (Järviluoma et al., 2011).

A motivating factor for signifying gender in this book and in our reflexivity and analysis is because middle classness for Blacks is a precarious position (Khunou, 2015a; Southall, 2016); it is difficult to define (Burger et al., 2015; Canham & Williams, 2017); and because other identity signifiers are also important for fully explaining social experiences and meaning making than class (Bettie, 2014; Gopalda, 2013). Gopalda (2013) also states that various identities matter including age, gender, citizenship, education, ethnicity, income, sexual orientation, socio-economic status, immigration and others. Therefore, it is important to note that each identity provides a different privilege and marginalisation in different contexts (Crenshaw, 1991). It is thus the contention of this book that gender as a category for analysis is significant for understanding how women and men of this class experience Black middle classness differently, and thus how the research team in particular, as members of communities that do gender, experienced the participants. Again, a gender analysis also provides a lens for understanding differences, as "gender does not act the same in all contexts" (Oyewumi, 2002).

Furthermore, we are interested in using gender as a category of reflexivity as it presents an opportunity to think about and comprehend the politics of representation as well as when and how we perform gender. For some scholars like Martin (2005) such reflexivity presents us with an opportunity to "catch gender in practice". This idea of catching gender in practice is premised on an understanding that gender includes positions that people occupy, and actions that people engage in (Martin, 2005; Oyewumi, 2002). This exercise has been useful for us as researchers to think about not only how our study participants shared varied experiences and conceptions of Black middle classness but also how we might have gendered them in our engagement during the interviews. Again, this reflexivity allowed us to think about how in our consideration of the phenomenon we were not only influenced by our identification with the class position but also by our identification with a particular gender.

PERFORMING MIDDLE CLASSNESS

Studies of class and social stratification have been useful in facilitating our understanding of how inequality is manifested. Most of these studies have, however, focused on how inequality is expressed or experienced from the perspective of gender, race and region. Again, as will be shown in chapters that follow, Black middle class studies in South Africa have focused mainly on education, income and occupation, and less on subjective measures, and, most importantly for this book, very little on physical appearance, dress and the interview process. How one dresses or acts in social settings with regards to accepting food, a ride or other "favours" is influenced by the individual's assumptions, beliefs, perceptions and feelings about themselves and those they are interacting with (Johnson, Lennon, & Rudd, 2014). Dress has been defined as a collection of adjustments used to "communicate and enact various identities" (Johnson et al., 2014; Kang, Sklar, & Johnson, 2011).

In the *Power of Looks: Social Stratification of Physical Appearance*, Berry (2016) argues that individuals who do not display the finest outfits or those whose appearance does not fit the norm experience prejudice and discrimination. She further asserts that looks matter because, "we gain and lose social power depending on our physical appearance" (Berry, 2016, p. 12). What is of relevance for this book is, however, that these impacts are not experienced the same by women and men. This book will therefore focus on how gender was experienced through dress, accepting food and transport, and experiencing discomfort during the interview process.

Even though early methodology textbooks prescribed that researchers are expected to be mere observers during interviews, this is not entirely true in the actual experience of interviews because researchers also "act" during the interview process (Mama, 2005). Researcher characteristics such as their age, race, ethnic group, class and gender have an impact on how the researcher appears in the research process, and that in turn influences the researcher's interaction with the participants. Lisiak (2015) suggests that researchers are active participants during interviews, as they bring in props, which assist them in performing their position as researchers. Tools that allow researchers to perform the researcher position include the voice recorder, notepads, cameras and interview guides among others. The use of these tools and the label of researcher indicate that the researcher poses a different embodiment during interviews, and this is evident in the way they talk and dress and their body language (Lisiak, 2015). This performance of the researcher position creates an impression of who they are (Lisiak, 2015).

Although having preconceived assumptions about the study participants and the phenomenon under investigation is inevitable, it is important to note that when these preconceived ideas are not critically engaged with, it creates challenges in the interview process. It is very common that researchers would have perceptions about their research participants. Lisiak (2015) argues that having assumptions as a researcher is essential; however, assumptions that are created should not be reducible to the participant because the assumptions the researcher might have about the respondent might not be true.

The Development of the Research Team and Collaboration

This research team began to form in 2014 when Professor Marsh applied for a new grant programme at the University of Maryland (UMD)[2]. In early 2014, Professor Marsh contacted Professor Khunou to see if the two could meet while she was in South Africa. Professor Marsh was aware of Professor Khunou's work on the Black middle class and was eager to see if there was any overlapping research interest and potential for collaborative projects. At the time Professor Marsh planned to travel to South Africa, she had already published several articles on the Black middle class in the Unites States of America and had secured a book contract with Cambridge University Press on members of the emerging Black middle class who are single and living alone. Professor Marsh wrote the proposal and Professor Khunou provided a letter of support for the grant. Professor Marsh was awarded the grant in April 2014 and the two stayed in contact over the next year.

In March 2015, Professor Marsh travelled to South Africa. Professor Khunou and Professor Marsh met and discussed several collaborative projects. One project discussed was the larger project this book is based on. The project was to use the personal narratives of the Black middle class to investigate the interrelationship between the middle class identity, long-term post-apartheid implications for racial and economic inequality, and neighbourhood context. This overarching theme divided into six manageable and interconnected themes: 1) defining the Black middle class; 2) spending patterns and lifestyles; 3) partnerships and gender; 4) politics; 5) neighbourhood choices and 6) overall well-being. During the 2015 visit, Professors Khunou and Marsh decided that Professor Marsh would return to America and write a Fulbright application to return to South Africa for a substantive amount of time.

In August 2015, Professor Marsh, with the assistance of and endorsement letter from Professor Khunou, submitted an application to the Fulbright United State Scholar Program. Professor Marsh was informed in March 2016 that she had been selected by the J. William Fulbright Foreign Scholarship Board for a Fulbright fellowship. Professors Khunou and Marsh continued to develop their project on the Black middle class.

In January 2017, Professor Marsh arrived in South Africa. Professors Khunou and Marsh officially started on their larger research agenda. By the end of the Fulbright, several activities were done. Professor Marsh established a Visiting Faculty position at the University of Johannesburg (UJ) and an additional Visiting Position at the University of Witwatersrand (a public research institution in Johannesburg), secured Institutional Review Board (IRB) approval for collaborative project through the UMD, *Conceptualizing the Black Middle Class in the South African context*, IRB Number: 1003010-1. Professor Khunou submitted and got the project ethics approval from the Faculty of Humanities Ethics Committee at the UJ.

Once in South Africa, Professors Marsh and Khunou recruited prospective study participants, building a database of 133 individuals. They put together the research team (the criteria for participation in the research team was that they should have at least a Master of Arts or be close to completing one, have an interest in building research careers, and have experience with research interviews), then developed the interview protocol. The protocol was then workshopped with several scholars of the Black middle class at UJ. This workshop was one of the multiple training workshops provided to the research team. Grace's National Research Foundation grant for rated scholars was used to host the workshops and for fieldwork transport. Once the protocol was finalised the four emerging scholars on the team conducted pilot interviews. The protocol was revised and finalised basis of these pilots interviews.

We then conducted 85 face to face interviews, described in more detail below. To monitor both issues of data saturation and positionality we met weekly during the fieldwork process and transcribed as we did the interviews. These weekly research team meetings debriefed and dealt with whatever issues might have come up during the week. Another reason for the weekly meetings was to make sure that we were able to identify when we were reaching data saturation. Fusch and Ness (2015) maintain that data saturation happens when a ceiling on the ability to obtain additional new information is reached. The weekly meetings were also a time to reflect on our experiences with the interviews and to think about how we are positioned and how we in turn position our participants (Mama, 2005). This book is based on the context of those weekly meetings.

In early 2018, upon her return to the United States, Professor Marsh together with Professor Khunou, applied for the Research and Service Award (RASA) through the UMD. The purpose of this grant was to bring the South African research team to the United States. Through funding from RASA and travel funding from the University of Johannesburg International and Research Office, we were able to come together again, in the United States context, to collaborate on analysing our qualitative data for this book and other writing projects. During this time, we wrote the book proposal and sample chapters for this book.

THE RESEARCH TEAM

The research team consisted of six people. Four were graduate students at the time of the study and for most of the writing time, while the two remaining members are co-principal investigators. Three members of the team are Black South

African women (one of the co-principal investigators and two students, all three born and raised in Soweto, Johannesburg). The other co-investigator is a Black American woman. The other two members of the team are Black men: one of Nigerian origins and the other a South African, also born in Soweto. By 2018, all members of the research team had an association with the UJ, the University of Witwatersrand or the UMD. Prior to this study, all team members had experience in qualitative research methods. The team had extensive practice and research experience working in Black communities in South Africa and America. The co-investigators started working together in 2014 and their professional relationship continues. Given the different socio-economic characteristics of the research team, it is important to "examine how their experiences shape their understanding of the interview experience and the data collection process" (Nduna, Sikweyiya, Khunou, Pambo, & Mdletshe, 2015).

All research team members demonstrated commitment to the research process and were asked to grapple with and reflect on their own socio-economic class identity relative to their interview participants. Most of the researchers on the team were "insiders" as South Africans but "outsiders" to the middle class position, which was beneficial as well as complicated and convoluted for a study of this nature.

Introducing our connection to the research is useful to allow the readers to better understand the lens through which we as researchers understand our research experiences. This also allows for the research team to overtly acknowledge, explain and review their biases throughout the research process (Lyons & Chipperfield, 2000). All members of the team brought an "insider" perspective (based on either the regional South African or middle class context, or identification with a particular gender) as well as an "outsider" perspective (based on us as academics, researchers and non-South Africans) to the project.

Grace: One of the co-principal investigators is a Sociology professor in a South African university. She is currently middle class but grew up in Soweto in a working-class family and most of her family members remain working class. She has written on the Black middle class and some of its various dimensions.

Kris: The other co-principal investigator is a 2017 Fulbright Scholar and faculty member in a North American university. She grew up middle class in the USA and studies the Black middle class. She acknowledged her North American privilege as a Fulbright in South Africa and did most of the initial recruiting for the study. This is reflected on in more detail later in the book.

Lesego: This female graduate-student team member grew up working class in Soweto and studied the experiences of single Black middle class women on intimate relationships in Soweto, Johannesburg. She still considers herself working class but acknowledges that her education is beginning to open up middle class experiences for her.

Polite: The other female graduate-student team member also grew up working class in Soweto and her current project looks at exploring the narratives of the lived experience of Black women who have been diagnosed with breast cancer in Gauteng. She still considers herself working class and holds a tension with regards to the existence of the Black middle class.

Leo: One of the male graduate students on the research team is a Nigerian of middle class status living in a middle class neighbourhood in Johannesburg and has a social network that is largely made up of middle class professionals. He is actively involved in researching young masculinities in Africa.

Mabone: The other male student is a working-to-middle class South African and studies the experiences of Black academics and their racial identity in white spaces. Although he acknowledges different economic positionalities for Blacks, he struggled with pinning down the idea of a Black middle class during this project.

The heterogeneous nature of the research team made for a rich and nuanced understanding of the interview process and provided various insider/outsider-standpoint perceptions on the nature of the term Black middle class and the larger research project.

STUDY DESIGN

As mentioned above, the six-person research team included two co-principal investigators, one being a Black South African professor and the other a Black American professor, and four Black post-graduate student researchers. The research team worked together to develop all aspects of the study design. Interviews were conducted in late-July and August 2017. Demographic information and identifiers of the participants (age, race, gender, occupation, highest level of education completed and names of their communities) were collected during the interviews. Table 1 provides the demographic details of the study participants.

The demographic statistics of the respondents are important to contextual the level of Black middle class respondents we interview. We administered a brief demographic survey to each respondent after the interview. The responses on the survey were put into a spreadsheet to calculate various demographic information.

The average age of the respondent was 38.6 years of age. The youngest member of the Black middle class we interviewed was 20 years of age. The oldest was 66 years

Table 1. Descriptive Statistics.

Measure	Percentage
Average age	38.6 (years)
Minimum age	20 (years)
Maximum age	66 (years)
Marital status	
Married	47%
Single	49%
Divorced	4%
Gender	
Female	64%
Male	36%
Nationality	
South Africa	90%
Zimbabwean	2%
United States of America	2%
Swaziland	1%
Malawi	1%
France	1%
Ethiopia	1%
Schools attended	
Public	50%
Private	25%
Public and private	25%
Highest level of education	
Advanced degree	77%
Bachelor's degree	15%
Certificate	7%
Current occupation	
Self-employed	22%
Manager/Director	31%

Table 1. (*Continued*)

Measure	Percentage
Banker	14%
Legal	5%
Medical field	6%
Entertainment	7%
Education	7%
Miscellaneous	7%
Assets	
Property	56%
Other investments	17%
Minimum income	20,000
Maximum income	150,000

of age. For marital status, 47% were married, 49% were single and only 4% were divorced.

The women respondents outnumber the men by almost a 2–1 ratio. Women made of 64% of the population compared to only 36% for men. We are not suggesting that more women are middle class than men. We are suggesting that women are more likely to respond to a request for an interview than men.

The vast majority of those we interviewed were from South Africa (90%). The remaining 10% of the population ranged from Zimbabwe, Swaziland, Malawi, Ethiopia the United States of America and France.

We asked the respondents, "What type of schools did you attend (private, public)?" Half of the members of the Black middle class that we interviewed went to public schools. A quarter (25%) attended private schools. The other quarter (25%) attended a combination of public and private institutions.

We then asked the highest level of education. We collapsed multiple education categories into three broad categories. "An advanced degree" is anything beyond a Bachelor's degree. "A Bachelor's degree" is those that graduated with this degree. "A Certificate" is anything the respondents wrote as an option. More than three-quarters (77%) of the respondents have advanced degrees. Less than 20% hold Bachelor's degree. Less than 10% have a certificate.

Similar to the education variable and based on the responses given, we collapsed the occupation responses into broader categories. For example, those respondents that noted they were Business Owners, Chief Executive Officers, Entrepreneurs, etc. we placed them in the broader category of "Self-Employed." Twenty-two percent (22%) of the population fall into the self-employed category. The largest occupation category includes those that are Managers and Directors. Those in the Banking and related occupation comprise 14% of the population. Those in the legal field are 5% followed by 6% in the medical field. Those respondents in entertainment, education and other occupations all tie for 7% of the overall population.

As for assets, more than half (56%) are property owners. In most case, this means they own (or are buying) their homes and 17% have additional assets and investments beyond property. The income range is wide. The minimum income is Rs. 20,000 while the maximum income is Rs. 150,000.

The interviews occurred in and around Johannesburg, South Africa. Johannesburg is the biggest city in South Africa and the capital of Gauteng. It is where most South African's and external migrants come for work and other economic opportunities. Johannesburg was the most suitable study site for understanding the Black middle class as it boosts the largest number of individuals who self-identify as Black middle class and this is true when using objective measures of Black middle class. Again, as compared to the rest of the country income ranges in Johannesburg are higher as compared to other cities. de Villiers (2019) illustrates that salaries in Johannesburg are on average Rs. 37,105 as compared to Cape Town which is at Rs. 32,153 and Durban which is at Rs. 25,020. According to the City of Johannesburg website, Johannesburg has a population of over 4 million with over 70% of the population being Black.

Participants were recruited from social gatherings, events and other settings, as well as through acquaintances and informal contacts. Interested participants were emailed to solidify the logistics (date, time and location) of the interview. The sample included participants who self-identified as African, Black-African and Coloured[3] who are somewhere on the spectrum of middle class. Our definition of Black in the book refers to all of these groupings. We interviewed 29 men and 52 women, with four pilot interviews making a total of 85 interviews. All interview participants were given pseudonyms to protect their identity. Audio recordings of the interviews were transcribed. The study received ethics clearance from the Faculty of Humanities Ethics committee at the University of Johannesburg and the IRB at the UMD. Thus, the following ethical principles were followed:

- voluntary participation
- informed consent
- doing no harm and
- confidentiality

According to Nduna et al. (2015), ethical principles are significant in social research as they allow researchers to maintain research integrity and to enhance the study findings. Similar principles informed our deliberation with the participants from conception to fieldwork and now as we engage with the data and the writing process.

At the end of the fieldwork process, we had completed 85 face-to-face interviews. Interviews ranged from 30 minutes to 120 minutes with an average time of 60 minutes. To determine participation in the study prospective participants had to self-identify as middle class, however in our engagement with them we took into account occupation, income and education as markers of middle classness. Transcription of interviews took place as each interview was completed and all 85 interviews were transcribed by a transcription company, which adheres to research ethical principles informing the study.

SYNOPSIS OF THE BOOK

In the discussion above we have illustrated that is difficult to come up with one conception of middle classness. This difficulty and the insider–outsider dynamics of doing research are the foundations for this book and inform our attempts to re-examine the knowledge production process. To achieve this endeavour the book presents the following chapters.

Chapter 2: The Black middle class: a conceptual moving target? The overarching theme of this chapter is situated in the experiences of interviewing the Black middle class within the theoretical framework of conceptualising the Black middle class. This chapter explores extending the definition of the Black middle class to include the experiences, perceptions and reflections of the researcher studying them. Including the voice of the researcher is an important dimension of studying socio-economic status and identities previously overlooked by most scholars.

Chapter 3: Those snobbish "clever" Blacks: preconceived notions of the Black middle class. This chapter examines the preconceived notions of the Black middle class held by the researchers before, after and during the interview process. This chapter also highlights how the researchers questioned their qualitative methodologies while taking responsibility for their insider/outsider positionality. Specifically, this chapter emphasises how the class status of the researchers influenced the interview process. This chapter takes the unique approach of sharing the personal experiences of the researchers in the research process. This unique look into the narratives of the researchers can improve understanding of the research enterprise and therefore data on the Black middle class. These reflections illustrate that interviewing the Black middle class is a complex, convoluted and evolving process.

Chapter 4: Thank you, but I got this: gender dynamics between researcher and Black middle class respondent. This explores the complexity of the gender dynamics between the researcher and their Black middle class respondents when trying to understand this demographic group. This book interweaves the gender dynamic of researcher and respondent with the well-documented multiple barriers to middle class status that Black people and women face.

Chapter 5: What do I wear, and do I eat their food? Performing middle classness. This chapter captures the richness of Black middle class individuals and their performance of middle classness from the perspective of the researcher and addresses the personal narratives from the research team about how they performed middle classness in the presence of their Black middle class respondents. Both components of this chapter are interrogated through the voices and reflections of the research team. This chapter demonstrates how history, theories and conceptualisations shape understandings of how to perform middle classness and how this production influences others to perform in a similar (or different) manner.

Chapter 6: Conclusion. It is clear from the researchers' narratives that studying the Black middle class can be challenging yet necessary to advance social science literature. Accordingly, this book makes four main contributions to social science. First, the book improves understanding of race and class in general, and of the Black middle class in particular. Second, it centralises the voices and perspectives of researchers when studying a hard-to-define demographic group. Third, it highlights how gender shapes our understanding of studying and defining the Black middle class. Fourth, it provides insight into ways to study and theorise the Black middle class for researchers.

NOTES

1. As part of the racial governance of apartheid South Africa, the homelands or what was referred to as Bantustans was the 13% of land reserved for Blacks to "govern" themselves.

2. The grant was The Global Partnership-Faculty Travel Grant. The purpose of the grant is to deepen the UMD's existing international connections, by funding travel to one or more existing UMD partner institutions to develop new collaborative projects and programmes, or to improve the implementation of

existing projects. The University of Johannesburg is a partner institution.

3. During apartheid, the different racial groups were divided into African, Indian Coloured. Our use of the term Black in this book includes African's, Coloured's and Indians to denote the shared oppression of these groups during apartheid and the continuing inequalities experienced by these groups.

2

THE BLACK MIDDLE CLASS: A CONCEPTUAL MOVING TARGET?

INTRODUCTION

Social science literature provides evidence that middle class status is precarious for Black populations who have achieved it. Apart from the collective discrimination and misconceptions that trail Black people as they move into middle class status, and how they are positioned vis-à-vis other race populations, scholars also grapple with who among Black populations should actually be considered middle class (Canham & Williams, 2017). As a result, Black middle class scholarship examines the breadth and depth of subjects ranging from marriage and mate selection, wealth accumulation, consumption patterns, participation in the arts, community mobilisation, political activism and social movements, to health and well-being, in an attempt to locate Black populations within middle class status. Yet the problem of defining the Black middle class is further compounded by the myriad ways and unstable manner in which Black population define themselves as middle class. These issues and the recent expansion of the numbers of those that consider themselves as members of the middle class in South Africa and abroad present scholars with an opportunity for inter-disciplinary scholarship (Spronk, 2016) and prospects for studying the global Black middle class.

A historical analysis of South African society illustrates that the Black middle class is not a new phenomenon (Mabandla, 2013; Ndletyana, 2014), as already discussed briefly in the previous chapter. In historical studies, this category encompassed the notions of a well-established Black middle class who were land owners, and mission educated (Bundy, 1988; Murray, 1992; Ndletyana, 2014; Peires, 1989). Later studies on the Black middle class focused on urban populations and centred their conception of the Black middle class through the lens of income and occupation, with an emphasis on managerial and professional categories (Crankshaw, 1997; Rivero, Du Toit, & Kotze, 2003; Seekings & Nattrass, 2006). After 1994, popular conceptions of Black middle classness centre on income, occupation and education (Visagie, 2013).

In this study, we understood that Blacks are not a monolithic group. The shared experience of Blackness is what Fanon (1952) refers to as the Fact of Blackness, where Blacks are "overdetermined from without". Therefore, the constructed fact of Blackness is overlooked also as this construction is based on a fixed notion of racist othering. Black, in apartheid racial categories in South Africa, positioned Indians, Africans and Coloureds within a differential hierarchy of Black. This classification was concerned with restricting and differentiating access to socio-economic resources, thus complicating what it means to be Black.[1]

The overarching objective of this chapter is to situate our reflections, as a research team, within the theoretical framework of the conceptualisation of the Black middle class. We explore such conceptualisations by examining a few conceptions presented by scholars studying the Black middle class. This chapter also captures nuances within the evolving definitions and conceptualisations of the Black middle class by analysing reflective narratives (generated from our last fieldwork meeting, which was recorded and transcribed) from our research team, which at times includes thoughts from our participants (generated during one on one interviews which were transcribed).

DISCUSSION OF FINDINGS: A CONCEPTUAL MOVING TARGET

This chapter explores the theme "The Black middle class: a conceptual moving target", as a reality faced by our research team in interviewing those who define themselves as Black and middle class. This chapter discusses four subthemes, which include 1. The more we learn the less we know; 2. Debt assaults middle class status; 3. Wealth sustains middle class status and 4. The struggle is real.

As illustrated in Chapter 1, scholars struggle to come to a consensus on how to define the Black middle class. Literature has evolved from objective to subjective to an amalgamation of objective and subjective measures, but the term remains a conceptual moving target. As a research team, we find ourselves grappling with similar issues and theoretically driven questions: How do we define the Black middle class? Are we members of the Black middle class? And should we continue to use the term Black middle class?

THE MORE WE LEARN THE LESS WE KNOW

The more we read as scholars, the more we learn. The more we interview those that define themselves as Black and middle class, the more we learn. The more we learn and centre the voices of the Black middle class, the less we know and equally seek to know. Polite provides a powerful narrative that bridges these subthemes that we as a team are trying to sort out as we conducted interviews and reflected on the interviews. Polite wrote:

> *The term 'Black middle class' is one that I have always found troubling and dislocated in the South African context. Middle class in South Africa is often defined as the emerging economic group, which is defined by their rising economic standing, their access to limited flexible credit and other resources. One of the most prominent currencies of the middle class is access to former racially segregate spaces, and having the best educational standing ... Despite how conflicted I feel about the 'term' Black middle class, it exists ... and remains at the center of South Africa's continuous transformation.*

Polite's dilemma with conceptions of the Black middle class is a common one for many South Africans. Khunou (2015a), in her article, titled *What Middle Class? The Shifting and Dynamic Nature of Class Position*, writes about how the precarious nature of the middle class position during apartheid and in contemporary South Africa leads to self-identification challenges and contributes to conceptual challenges with the term. When Polite says, "*Despite how conflicted I feel about the 'term' Black middle class, it exists*", it illustrates how the term remains in flux, and her constant engagement with what it means. Polite's dilemma is confounded by the fact that the participants she interviewed also shared contradictory conceptions. One of her participants defined the Black middle class in the following ways;

> *As the people who can easily afford the basic necessities without any efforts.... Yeah, I think with the black Middle class the biggest challenge is the concept of black tax, right?...And as much as there are certain things we can afford like food, vehicles, access to funding from a finance perspective, um, access to property ownership, uh, but I really think, uh, the definition differs for White middle class.*
> (Interview 1PC)

While Polite's first participant initially argues that affordability is without effort, she later indicates that there is the issue of Black tax which is a result of the country's racial inequality which still enables more resources and privilege to accrue to Whites. Although the term "Black Tax" has been negatively appropriated in media discourses, for most of our participants it indicated that Blacks in the middle class had an unequal share of responsibility to kin compared to other racial groups as a result of South Africa's racist past and limited state social security. Ndinga-Nyanga (2019) argues that uncritical use of the term Black Tax tends to empty out the continued reciprocal care work that Blacks continue to do for their kin, and further argues that, this care work does the real work of income redistribution, as social security is unequal and limited.

While Polite was still grappling with this conception, her second participant offered another layer to the conception:

> *I don't know if transcended is the right word to use, but transcended from the oppressions that Black*

> *people were put in, in the past, or just transcended from what the Black ... the typical Black person was supposed to be.* (Interview 2PC)

Although there is a bit of resonance between the two conceptions, the differences are stark and, for Polite – someone who is already sceptical about the existence of the middle class among Blacks – this compounded her challenge, as Polite holds the idea that, given the precarious nature of this class position, it should not even be considered a position.

It was, therefore, not a surprise that even though Leo did not come to the research with a background on studying the Black middle class, and only had a general knowledge of how middle classness was defined in the social science literature, his experience also illustrated the challenge of this fluidity of the term. During and after the fieldwork, Leo felt the term was "*a moving target*": the more he interviewed respondents, the more he was sure of this moving target. He reflected on comments he made in our post-fieldwork meetings that captured the essence of this moving target. In a slightly frustrated vain, Leo notes the slippery nature and fluidity of the term middle class by saying that,

> *One moment, I am talking to a participant and I say to myself: "Eureka!" Then I go for the next interview and eureka disappears as quickly as it entered into my head.*

What Leo is suggesting in the above quote, and what the rest of the research team echoes, is that the more we learn about defining the Black middle class the less we actually know how to define this demographic group. Again, in our review of both South African and international literature, we realise that we can talk to ten different academics and get ten different definitions of the Black middle class and the same is true when we interview ten different members of the Black middle class. From this dilemma, it is apparent that diverse nuanced conceptions of what it means to be Black middle class should be foregrounded in studies of the Black middle class. Such a centring will also be useful for further theorising of this concept. The following are a few of the definitions that came from the participants interviewed by Leo:

> *In general, I define the Black middle class as those who are just emerging into those new markets, who can afford basics such as buying homes, cars, and access to decent education.* (Interview 1LI)
>
> *...I'd say the Black middle class is a ... financial category.* (Interview 2LI)
>
> *I would define it as people who can get by, and can afford a couple of luxuries.* (Interview 3LI)

Even though these definitions vary, what remains constant among the members of the Black middle class we interviewed is that they capture how this class position allows for access to the basics. However, what is most important in conceptions of the Black middle class is that membership of this class position does not provide a protective measure against their racial identity. The Black middle class as a demographic group and as individuals are still victims of racism and discrimination. In the 1980s, following in the footsteps of the colonial rulers, the apartheid state, in an attempt to maintain apartheid, put forward measures to create a Black middle class as a social buffer – thus differentiating between well-off, educated Blacks and poor, working-class Blacks. To say there is a Black middle class is to contest the Black imagery and the idea that the collective Black experience is nothing more than a poor experience. Put another way, to suggest there is a Black middle class refutes this normative narrative that all Blacks are poor and/or live the poor experience. The concept of Black and middle class is a dilemma for a White supremacist structure. In her articulation of how apartheid racist politics reduced Blackness to poverty, Posel (2010) illustrates how the possibility of access to social and economic resources for Blacks is counter to apartheid's conceptions of Whiteness.

As a research team, we still struggle with Black middle class definition(s) before, during, and after interviews. We are starting to see the empirical and theoretical value in defining (or deciding to not put strict parameters on defining) the Black middle class. Leo draws from an interaction with a Professor he interviewed, who we will call Jane, to serve as part of the foundation for his own evolving definition of the Black middle class – a definition that still holds points of apprehension. Leo discussed how, after his interview with Jane ended and the audio-recorder was off, she asked him two very direct questions: first, *"What's your hypothesis thus far about the middle class?"* and second, *"How would you define them?"* In a mildly funny but all too familiar episode for academics when asked questions which they are not prepared to answer, Leo explains how he struggled to provide adequate answers while at the same time previous interviews were resonating in his mind. At that point, Leo realised he *"had in fact been trying to pin down a definition with no success"*. Leo goes on to reflect that:

> *If anyone asked me for a definition of the middle class now, I would probably give the same response as I did to Professor Jane. I am not sure that frustration is the word I ought to use, but I did experience this sometimes as the question tormented me. I continually asked myself what we were going to pin down at the end of the project; what were we going to come up with*

> *about a definition of the middleclass? I had no answers and remember having this feeling at the back of my mind whether the project was going to have any theoretical value. Thinking about it now, perhaps it does have research value in terms of me appreciating that seeking an encompassing definition of the middle class that would apply to all individuals is elusive and a futile exercise. Still, I don't know!*

As a research team, we share Leo's sentiments and frustrations. Khunou (2015a) – captures the dilemma aptly; even though in this article Khunou grapples with the precarious existence of this class position for Blacks, her research experience and further engagement in this project provides further, similar, questions – *what middle class?* In the interviews she conducted, a few made her go back to her meditations when writing the 2015 article.

As an American, Kris reflects on some of her experiences interviewing the Black middle class in America compared to South Africa and how these previous interactions shape some of her preconceived notions. While analysing the narratives for her forthcoming book, "The Love Jones Cohort: Single and Living Alone in the Black Middle Class" (Cambridge University Press), Kris and her American research team were aware of two interesting and related philosophies kept emerging: DuBois's theory of the "Talented Tenth" and the marketing moguls' mantra of "keeping up with the Joneses". But these two philosophies are based on separate and competing ideas. The philosophy for the Talented Tenth, as noted (but later rejected) by DuBois is that

> *The Negro race, like all races, is going to be saved by its exceptional men. The problem of education, then, among [them they] must first of all deal with*

> *the Talented Tenth; it is the problem of developing the Best of this race that they may guide the Mass away from the contamination and death of the Worst, in their own and other races.*

DuBois' vision, then, was that having the capacity to be one of the Talented Tenth and being of the Black middle class meant taking care of those less fortunate than yourself and working to uplift the entire Black community. Conversely, the philosophy of "keeping up with the Joneses" refers to

> *the comparison to one's neighbor as a benchmark for social class or the accumulation of material goods. To fail to 'keep up with the Joneses' is perceived as demonstrating socio-economic or cultural inferiority.*

In this age of consumerism, in which many people define themselves by what they possess, the philosophy is one of self-interest and conspicuous consumption. The respondents in Kris's American research project, seem to have internalised DuBois' ideology of the Talented Tenth, because the idea of being Black and middle class to them is inextricably linked to the responsibility to uplift the Black masses. Many respondents in the South African study suggested the Black middle class have to pay a Black tax. In the American context, Black tax often means the Black middle class have to work harder than the other people and still get the same or less pay. Kris acknowledges that she had some preconceived notions that American scholarship on the Black middle class would be universal. However, she found that slightly different terms were used to express similar ideas. For example, middle class Black South Africans also mentioned a Black tax but in a slightly different context. For South Africans, Black tax was more about the responsibility to take care of the larger Black community in a context of continued precarity.

The more we learn about the definition the more we realise we have so much more to learn. Furthermore, the moving-target nature of the term causes us to question if there is value in continuing to study this group and trying to pin down the term. Then we have to step back, reflect and understand that, as scholars, we are doing much more than continually fighting to define the term. We, as scholars, are highlighting and forcing others to acknowledge that Blacks, based on the history of race in South Africa and globally, are constantly wrestling with their potential middle class status and all the implications, consequences, advantages and contradictions of being Black and middle class.

As we continue to examine, evaluate, interrogate and understand the Black middle class in South Africa, and globally, we find two stubbornly, consistent empirical facts present in the social science literature and our research findings. First, as a collective and global group, middle class Blacks continue to face historical and persistent marginalisation, discrimination and segregation. Second, the global Black middle class is making some, albeit extremely modest, social mobility strides (Krige, 2012), while a class of impoverished Blacks falls further and further behind (Alexander, Ceruti, Motseke, Phadi, & Wale, 2013). These large and persistent inequities between the Black and White middle classes, as well as scholarly disagreement over the definition of the class, should continue to lead scholars to question, explore and continually take a critical view of the very existence of, and/or assume the fragility of, a Black middle class in South Africa and abroad.

Debt Assaults Middle Class Status

Debt is a concept that often comes up when discussing the Black middle class, both in the literature, among our respondents and in our preconceived ideas on what middle class experiences are about (James, 2014; Krige, 2011; Mattes, 2002). It is, first, important to situate debt within the larger narrative of financial literacy that we as a research team discussed. During the final fieldwork meeting, Mabone provided an expressive overview of financial literacy:

> *An expected and uncomfortable component of the data collection and interaction with the participants was the idea of middle class existence. As a research assistant I had to ponder my financial literacy. Their [the study participants] experiences and perceptions on financial management were distressing and impacted my analysis of myself. The [Black middle class] conveyed a financial prudency I lacked. I felt as if I was learning as they spoke of both financial mismanagement and proper planning, it always became an introspective aspect of data collection. I felt uneasy in each interview - I experienced how I was depriving myself of the [Black middle class] comforts because of my financial illiteracy.*

Financial literacy, credit scores and debt are interrelated words that come up when discussing the general identity of the middle class. Like various other concepts, financial literacy is also defined in different ways by those who do research on it; these multiple conceptions include the following aspects; "(a) a specific form of knowledge, (b) the ability or skills to apply that knowledge, (c) perceived knowledge, (d) good financial behavior, and even (e) financial experience" (Hung, Andrew, Parker, & Yoong, 2009). The assumption Mabone is making in the above quote is that those who are more financially literate, that is, those who have the financial knowledge and use it in their financial decision making (Hung et al., 2009), will make better money-related decisions, avoid debt and ultimately end up with better credit scores that allow for more wealth-building opportunities. Mabone even acknowledges some of these notions himself by writing the following statement in his reflexive fieldnotes:

> *However, what stood out for me was the fact that I saw the link of education and financial literacy as means of maintaining [Black middle class] status. I could interact freely with the views on education, but my use of money consistently made me feel as if I was being taught and I listened. I was exposed! I did not have financial literacy; I felt I was wasteful with money. But, the engagements exposed the truth; I did not know money, or its value. The participants did, this was laid bare for me to see in the data collection. Finance and how to use it clearly separated me from the participants; I was left to reflect on how my money is misused, I got an education I had not considered.*

Financial education in the South African context is a trial and error endeavour for the poor and the emerging Black middle class. The education system does not offer it and financial institutions pretend to offer it in their endeavours to sell financial products to South Africans. According to Robert et al (2012, p. 18) in the South African Financial Literacy report,

> *a clear class and human capital bias was evident. The groups with the highest financial literacy score were: the tertiary educated, the wealthy, those in fulltime employment and residents in formal urban areas.*

This clearly shows that the inequality in the country influences wealth creation in multiple ways.

Although financial literacy is an important aspect of both personal wealth building and institutional financial management, it is not the only aspect for wealth building. We want to be clear that equal access to opportunities and resources plays an important role in whether money will be earned, kept and grown into various measures of wealth.

However, what is obvious is that racial inequality still plays a role in how resources are allocated. The assumption should not be that the processes for accessing financial education and resources are open, fair and accessible to all people regardless of their race, ethnicity or gender. We know this is not the case. When scholars look at financial literacy they should interrogate how racism and discrimination factor into which racial and ethnic groups are steered into large amounts of debt. It is also important to acknowledge that credit was not easily accessible to Blacks during apartheid, thus making it difficult for them to operate fully in the market economy. Again, financial literacy and the indebtedness of the Black middle class should be interrogated in a context that clearly appreciates that wealth building is intergenerational and that the emerging Black middle class does not have access to that intergenerational wealth.

For an example of the structural forces that fuel racial wealth disparities, we turn to banking. There have been recent claims that South African banks have been charging Black consumers higher interest rates on mortgage loans than their White counterparts (Ryan, 2018). This racialisation contributes to the financial standing of the Black middle class, how they experience and are able to deal with debt, and in turn how they understand their positioning as members of the middle class.

Given the global racial context, one important and in some ways unavoidable aspect of the evolving definition of the Black middle class, whether in South Africa, America or in general, is that any definition is subjected to the assault of debt. It could be argued that the term Black middle class is an oxymoron. Being Black and middle class are contradictory terms that cancel each other out, based on the omnipresent debt that Blacks face globally. While, both historical (Frazier, 1957; Veblen, 1899) and contemporary scholars (Seekings, 2010; Southall, 2016) either directly or indirectly address the notion of debt through the concept of conspicuous consumption; that is purchasing expensive items as an outward display of social and socio-economic identity. The point is that this form of consumption is based on assumptions that the Black middle class are unable to afford such items and are willing to go into debt to secure such accoutrements. Mabone's submission that:

> *... The engagements exposed the truth; I did not know money, or its value. The participants did, this was laid bare for me to see in the data collection. Finance and how to use it clearly separated me from the participants; I was left to reflect on how my money is misused*

The above quote from Mabone indicates clearly that the participants had a money sense, which is not reflected in the conspicuous consumption narrative. In our initial analysis of the interviews, it became clear that age was an important determinant for financial management and debt levels of our participants, the older participants shared experiences of wealth building whereas the younger ones illustrated that they were still at a stage in their lives where they were making ends meet. Roberts et al. (2012) indicate that in their survey analysis on financial literacy in South Africa the young were positioned differently to older individuals. They argued that "young people in South Africa are inexperienced with regard to financial products, probably owing to their limited access to financial resources and their lack of a regular income" (Roberts et al., 2012, p. 18). This could explain why Mabone felt that he was less experienced about money management and that the interviews he had were a lesson on wealth building and financial management. Leo also discusses how the concept of debt came up with his participants,

> ... I recalled my conversations with some participants who told me that the [Black middle class] in South Africa is a confused bunch of people who are heavily indebted.

Thus, while we refute any sweeping conspicuous consumption characterisation of the Black middle class, we underscore how some members of this demographic are conscious of their adverse relationship with debt as they attempt to define themselves as middle class. Grace's questions about "*what middle class?*" were further heightened by encounters with participants' ideas on debt and its centrality to conceptions of the Black middle class. One of the participants interviewed by Grace made the following interesting observation on what it means to be middle class and Black;

> Borderline. Middle class live on debt. We, we drive in cars that we don't own. Okay? We have mobile phones that we're paying forever and they're said to be free when they're not really free. Uh, we live in property that we actually, um, belongs to the bank and the bank keeps us wanting more from it because they also give us what is called, uh, access bonds so you have, you can borrow against your own bond, uh, which then means you remain indebted. (Interview, 1GK)

The above quote speaks to the tenuous position of Black middle class where access to debt might remain an unending circle. The quote makes a note of how financial products are tailored to trap them into a circle of debt, and thus inability to build wealth. To illustrate how a lack of generational wealth traps and defines middle classness for Black participants, 1GK also said the following to illustrate this point;

> *But I mean if, if I could be kicked out, I would be out. (Laughs).* (Interview 1GK)

The above captures clearly how precarious the position of being Black and middle class is. On a similar note, Polite challenged the idea that there is a Black middle class because of the contradictions in terms of how they are portrayed as a growing significant class and the unending credit linked to their existence. She provides a powerful narrative that bridges the debt and education notions that we as a team struggled with as we conducted interviews and reflected on them afterwards. Polite writes

> *The term "Black middle class" is one that I have always found troubling and dislocated in the South African context. Middle class in South Africa is often defined as the emerging economic group, which is defined by their rising economic standing, their access to limited credit and other resources.*

Access to credit as indicated by Polite is central to how the middle class in South Africa was created. However, what is challenging with recent analysis of the Black middle class and debt is its removal from the historical racist context of the country and its continuities with regards to unequal ownership of banks, access to credit and the cultural capital linked to succeeding in the middle class position. Even though Polite was very critical of the structural challenges facing the middle class, in her reflections at the end of the fieldwork she, like Mabone, had the following to say about what she personally learned from interviews with this class about money:

> *So it became an eye opener that sometimes, we don't form to the middle class not because we don't have the ability, but it's how we using the money that's preventing us. And something all of them had in common is that they actually know how to use money [and] the value of everything.*

Even though there was an agreement that structural inequalities were a major deterrent for the Black middle class's growth and financial stability, Polite learned some interesting money management lessons from the interviews.

In our analysis of the findings, an important finding was on generational differences. The older participants had better money management skills and illustrated some experience with dealing with the unequal structure in ways that helped them build wealth in ways they had been unable to when they first entered the class and largely in ways that the younger participants were unable to. This ability to shift might have also been a result of the socio-economic conditions of that time, the younger emerging Black middle class are contending with different challenges including those influenced by social media and different values.

Wealth Sustains Middle Class Status

On the one hand, scholars must include debt (or lack thereof) when defining the Black middle class. On the other hand, social science literature admonishes scholars to include some type of wealth indicator, measured by assets, to define middle class groups, and the Black middle class should be no different.

One of our research team members, Lesego, had preconceived notions that cars, and expensive ones at that, were required for membership of the Black middle class position. Not until she had an interview with respondents who we will call Sheila and Denise, did Lesego consider reconceptualising aspects of this Black middle class definition. Lesego reflects on her thinking as she recounts her interaction with the two women on separate occasions. She shares:

> *I was shocked when one of the participants [Sheila] had mentioned that they do not own a car but then their annual income was above R500 000 a year. I had assumed that for middle class people, having a car is a necessity and especially having an expensive car. I questioned this woman's middle classness because Sheila did not have a car.*

Lesego was flabbergasted that someone without a car would define herself as middle class. Leo also encountered similar interviews where seemingly well-placed respondents in the Black middle class do not own cars. This was troubling and counter-intuitive to Lesego's preconceived understanding of a middle class identity until she critically examined an interaction she had with Denise. In our reflexive meeting she shared the following;

> *I also got confused though with Denise whom I had interviewed, who owns an old Corolla, but she was living in a big and beautiful house and she did not have a problem with driving an old car, as Denise was more focused on being financially comfortable. Denise had paid off her house and argued that she would rather invest in her property rather than a car because there is no value in a car as it depreciates. The perceptions I had, would be that*

> *for one to be middle class, they have to have cars, money, expensive clothes and this is not entirely true for everyone*

Popular and market research conceptions of what it means to Black and middle class suggests that engaging in visible consumption of things such as expensive cars and clothes are important markers of middle classness for Blacks at the expense of consumption of invisible wealth such as a house, investments and other subtler acquisitions. Ownership of a house, particularly in the suburbs, is seen as an indicator of social progression whereas renovating a house in the township is problematised as conspicuous consumption as the township is seen as a place that is downtrodden and not conducive to life (de Coninck, 2017; Krige, 2012). Thinking more about wealth, Lesego makes a subtle but powerful assessment about home-ownership as a possible and necessary indicator that should be considered in the middle class definition. Lesego reflected in the following ways on this;

> *Where I come from, before my dad had lost his job when I was young, if you could have asked my family's class status, the word middle class might have come up because we always believed that we were "neither rich nor poor". But come to think of it now since I am educated, that is really not enough. My dad could not buy himself a car when he was working, he could not buy himself a house or even move out from his mother's home. The only time my dad could renovate his house was when he got his retrenchment package, then how would that have made us middle class?*

For Lesego, her father's lack of wealth, shown in his inability to buy a house or a car, raises questions about how to classify her family and herself as middle class. Lesego's assessment affirms Polite's belief about the questionable nature of the conception, in her reflections, Polite argued that:

> *Middle class is an experience... it is not a position. For me, what is called middle class is an experience that is not guaranteed, that is not constant, that can be taken away any time. It is something for sale, where you purchase the lifestyle and hope that the chips do not come falling down on you.*

Polite's reflection in the above quote speaks to the precarity of the position. Saying it is *"something for sale"* is a powerful narrative as it illustrates that once you lose purchasing power then the experience is taken away from you. While a part of Lesego's life appears middle class through access to education, another part of her life does not include home or car ownership, which seems to exclude her family from the middle class category.

Similarly, Leo provides a critical reflection on why wealth, and even other standardised measures of middle classness, is relevant to a Black middle class definition. He discusses his interview with Bob, one of the first participants he interviewed. Bob co-owns a business and makes nearly R60 000 annually. In his reflection Leo illustrates the following:

> *... I struggled to come to terms with how Bob, ... said he earned R56 000 a year from a personal business he co-owned with a friend, could claim a middleclass position with those that earned half a million, over 1.5 million and so on. I continually asked myself whether Bob was actually referring to this annual income or something else to claim middle classness. But, what would that something be? When I asked him about what assets he*

> *owned, he explained to me that he had no assets whatsoever. What? Not even a car? No! Education-wise, he had a diploma in Financial Information Systems, and from my own thinking at the time this was the only evidence I could provide for any claim of his to middle class positioning. Yet, can a claim to middleclass positioning be hinged only on a diploma or education in general? Perhaps, this was a biased standpoint in my mental work. Indeed, I found myself comparing this participant not only to other participants but also to myself. For instance, I remember thinking that even I earned almost three times as much as he did from my student scholarship. Thus, while other participants' claim to middle classness made 'sense' to me, Bob's seemed unreal as far as a definition of middle classness is concerned. But, maybe it was not supposed to make sense to me even as I spent my entire conversation with him and thereafter thinking about this.*

In the above quote, education is viewed as limited without income to back it up. Thus, income is shown to be an important factor to consider when thinking about the Black middle class. As Leo and the rest of us as a team struggled to determine what matrix should be used for measuring the class identity of our respondents, we as a team start to solidify aspects of our own social identity. Take Lesego, for example: from her reflections she notes,

> *… I refuse to define myself as middle class and this is because I do not have wealth under my name even though I am educated, [more] highly educated than most participants that I had interviewed. However, I still do not regard myself as one of them and this is because I do not have the financial capacity to define myself as Black middle class.*

For the rest of the team, as we interviewed people along the entire spectrum of middle class, from entry level to "highly privileged" members of the Black middle class, we all had to continually take a step back as we reviewed our interviews, or to put it more accurately, engage in a "conceptual tap-dance". We found ourselves constantly reflecting on and taking a critical view of our own socio-economic identities. For example, Grace felt troubled after a few of her interviews with upper middle class participants, she reflected that:

> *I was uncomfortable as the promise of education was not illustrated in my lifestyle and my buying power. I used to think I was middle class, but after interviews with these high- income earners who were sometimes younger and without as many degrees as I have, I started rethinking.*

So, education without matching income makes the idea of middle classness shaky. It felt like after one interview we might feel confident in our self-reported class status but after the very next interview, we were back to questioning if we are middle class at all. The conceptual tap-dance continues.

The Struggle is Real

What is clear among the research team is that everyone is struggling with what is middle class from classical theorists like Karl Marx and Max Weber to contemporary scholars globally. Marx and Weber's work illustrate early attempts to understand how classes and middle classes manifest and are experienced in British society. Their work continues to influence contemporary ideas about middle classness in South Africa and globally (Alexander et al., 2013; Southall, 2016). While a debate rages on between such theorists, a similar debate happens between the respondent's answers. Likewise, we share similar notions in our mind: are we middle class and what does the term really mean? Lesego writes:

I grappled with trying to define the middle class and I still do and this is because there is no accurate definition for the term. When I am asked what the definition of the middle class is, I have to explain the whole debate of the meaning of the Black middle class. Even after the project the question still arises what is middle class? Participants grappled with it also and I could see that it was one term that they could not easily define and would in return ask me.

For example, several participants asked Lesego the following questions or gave the following responses after her question, "How do you define black middle class?"

1. "I actually don't know. (laughs) I actually don't know" (Interview 1LL).

2. "Um, this a very, uh, complicated question in South Africa (Interview 3LL).

3. "I don't know what that is. I don't know what that is. I don't believe in class."(Interview 4LL).

The dilemmas of being able to define the term were at times influenced by the fact that even though the participants fit the categories of income, education and occupation and volunteered to participate in the study they still felt there were challenges with the term. Like Lesego, Grace experienced a similar dilemma with one of her participants who responded like this to the concept question:

They can afford taking their children to private schools. They can afford holidays, you know?

> *Things like that. That's how I define black middle class. But, as I said before, I've never thought of myself as, or I've never classified myself. For me, I'm just living, just working, doing this and that... Wear what I can afford and that's it. I've never like really thought of myself as "Oh, I'm middle class." Or ... I know I'm not poor, but yeah, I've never really classified myself any way. (Interview 8GK)*

As researchers engaged in studying the Black middle class and what it means, at times we find ourselves uncomfortable with the self-definitions middle class respondents were giving during the interviews. From our research team reflections and post-interview meetings, there are many reasons why we sit in moments of discomfort across the table from our respondents. Is it that we are not middle class? Is it that we are not sure if a Black middle class exists and can be defined? Are we challenging any preconceived notions of the Black middle class or questioning if our middle class performance (or lack thereof) is clear to the respondent (see the chapter on *What do I wear and do I eat their food? Performing middle classness* for additional information)? Do we have additional questions running through our minds? Or, perhaps, our discomfiture as a team is a combination of all of the above? After our post-interview meetings, one question or concern that we all shared during the interview process was: what if the respondent wanted us to provide our own definition of the middle class? Would we be able to provide a clear, concise and coherent definition? Our education provides us not only with opportunities but also we have the burden of being the expert in the interviewer/interviewee power dynamics.

All research team members have advanced degrees, making us highly educated. However, in many cases, we made less money and had less wealth than those we interviewed.

They were middle class and wealthy but some paled in comparison to our educational aspirations and achievements; yet all of us struggled to reconcile in our minds how we are highly educated but located on the fringes, or barely able to confidently consider ourselves middle class. Mabone, Lesego and Leo capture this struggle the best with the following arratives. Mabone notes the following:

We were all to a degree educated but I felt I was an oddity… My qualification or studies allowed me to interact and have a level of authority that they recognized and I did not expect, they had interest in my thoughts. I anticipated I would have been asking them their views and be intrigued by what they read more than they would be in me.

In Mabone's case education became a safety net that allowed access to the participants. Being educated ensured there was a pointed of contact, a reference in which Mabone and the participants found commonalities, which eased any potential tensions in the research process. It made the environment and the research space enabling for discussion and open engagement. The middle ground that education brought allowed for an honest research process, there was a point of contact that eased the interviewee and interviewer relationship. Lesego provided a similar narrative to the one Mabone provides. She reflected that:

Participants would ask about what my vocation was before the interview and I would tell them that I am doing my master's and there was a bit of shock in it, because I was younger than most and they assumed that I am middle class. I mean I looked middle class because I dressed up like a middle class person and I was educated and was associated with Prof Kris

> *who is an American professor, so they assumed*
> *I was one of them. But was I really?*

An interesting observation made by Lesego above is around dress and middle classness and will be explained in more detail in a later chapter. Given the racialised conception of class in South Africa during apartheid, dress and how one looks are outward markers used to determine one's class position (Posel, 2010). Of the three, Leo had the most direct observation when he discussed an internal debate with himself about Bob, which we shared earlier in this chapter. Leo questioned how Bob could define himself as middle class, while he, Leo would soon be awarded a PhD and his graduate student scholarship was nearly three times more than Bob's annual income. In addition, while Bob called himself middle class, Leo, who was just shy of his PhD during this research project, does not question his middle class status but questions where he is on the middle class spectrum.

As a research team, we appeared to use our educational achievements as some sort of protective measure to feel comfortable and empowered in interviewing the middle class, while we internally struggled to understand how this did not necessarily translate into middle class status, at least from an economic standpoint. Mabone reflected thus;

> *Education was a fascinating discussion point;*
> *the participants and I had a similar outlook.*
> *It was valuable and a means of developing on*
> *the intelligence they naturally had. I related, it*
> *was not a Black middle class experience solely*
> *but a love of self-growth. The assertions and*
> *articulations - I found them applicable to my*
> *outlooks. There was an ease that I found in doing*
> *things the right way. Education is a means of*
> *self-sustenance. The fact that education was not*

just an exercise of obtaining certification but rather an exercise of development was important to me. It was relevant to the independence I had, as I too did not like things done for me. Education was freedom, it was beyond wealth. Therefore, obtaining information, passing and learning were core parts we found agreement in. The fact that I was "educated" made the discussions easier. I felt as if they could speak about it in detail because they knew I understood their view points, what they expressed about themselves and their children's education was similar to my outlook and experiences.

Considering Mabone's assertion above that education *"was beyond wealth"* one may suggest that this, and indeed the educational achievements of other team members, was a safety blanket, or a form of cultural capital, that we drew on to maneuver middle class positioning and identity. Indeed, we can reflect on Bourdieu's (1986) conception of cultural capital and how this grounds the confidence, competence and self-esteem that education offered us to see ourselves within this demographic. Yet, we also felt that we were not solidly middle class even as we attempted to perform this identity in the presence of those we interviewed.

While interacting with the Black middle class, Polite, despite her scepticism around the middle class, believed that education is vital for the development of the Black society. She recalls her interaction with some of her participants, indicating that education is a currency; she recalls an off the record conversation: *"One of the participants asserted that education is a currency that no-one defines for you but yourself".*

The issue of education made Polite reconsider her initial view of the Black middle class as comfortable and having "arrived". At the last meeting of the fieldwork she reflected thus on this issue:

> *Not only that are they intelligent, like when you speak to them. Is this thing of education I didn't expect from them. I thought, they were already comfortable. [it] is fine. But, all of them say "No, I can go back and study and see my children, they all go to government schools … So education became, I don't know, something that so concrete, it's beyond getting a job … but it's about developing yourself as a person of honesty. Even if the job goes away, I can get another job 'cause I'm qualified; I've gone to school … so [it] does give us something to think about because of school … But for them, always developing yourself, always learning.*

This interaction was interesting and significant for Polite as a young scholar in the making, that when one defines oneself as middle class it is about pursuing more than just material goods but also about acquiring something that no one can take away from you, which is education.

Lesego, Mabone and Polite highlight the importance of education as a self-serving privilege that benefits the individuals and the class itself. Historically, it was also evident how the Black middle class prided themselves on education, as, at the time, it afforded them opportunities compared to those who were less educated (Southall, 2016).

CONCLUSION

This chapter has discussed four main issues in an attempt to illustrate the complexities in conceptions of the Black middle class and the elusive and conceptually moving target of the term. These discussions were drawn from our research experiences of the Black middle class in South Africa. The four issues discussed in the chapter include an engagement with the conceptual challenges in work on the Black middle class; the problematic link between the Black middle class and debt; the significance of thinking about income and most importantly wealth in conceptions of Black middle classness; and finally, the chapter grappled with the constant and continuing challenge in defining what it means to be Black and middle class.

By looking at our own difficulties with conceptualising and self-identification with the Black middle class position, this chapter has contributed to the on-going debates about conceptualising the Black middle class in a way that is more nuanced. This discussion of our own personal engagement with the term as we were partaking in the interview processes provides an opportunity to think differently about theory building in Black middle class studies.

NOTE

1. For our study, when we use the term Black or Blacks, please see chapter 1 for a detailed explanation.

3

THOSE SNOBBISH "CLEVER" BLACKS: PRECONCEIVED NOTIONS OF THE BLACK MIDDLE CLASS

INTRODUCTION

This chapter reflects on our engagement with our own class status and preconceived notions of the Black middle class in the interview process in our study on the Black middle class. This chapter also engages with questions around the existence of the Black middle class and issues around the Blackness of the Black middle class, to illustrate how preconceived ideas were dealt with and how, with contact, these predetermined and at times narrow-minded notions changed. The reflections of the researchers illustrate that interviewing the Black middle class was a complex and evolving process. The chapter, in its engagement with preconceived ideas of those we study, also unpacks how the insider/outsider dynamic complicates the ways in which our preconceived ideas about our participants manifest.

This chapter focuses on how researchers' preconceived ideas about those they study affect how they engage with them and therefore the researchers' findings. We are no different as a research team. The discussions in the chapter centre particularly on how researchers' preconceived ideas influence qualitative studies on the Black middle class. Such reflections are significant for studies on the Black middle class especially in under-researched areas such as South Africa. Reflective considerations of the impact of preconceived ideas in projects on the Black middle class are important for re-examining knowledge production, for providing new humanising methods for dealing with these at the initial stages of the project and throughout the research.

Historically, there have been various policies implemented across the world with the goal of increasing social mobility of Blacks and potentially shaping a robust global Black middle class. In the early 1990s, with the end of apartheid and the birth of democracy in South Africa, the nation saw a rise in the Black middle class. These developments have seen an emergence of a Black middle class with access to class mobility, socio-economic resources and opportunities within a historically White lifestyle. Yet the South African Black middle class seems to have achieved social mobility but not social integration, as prejudice, discrimination and segregation are still part of their lives (Ndinga-Nyanga, 2019; Ndletyana, 2014). Furthermore, the Black middle class continues to exist in and to have to navigate societies that have preconceived ideas about them (Canham & Williams, 2017; Leopeng & Langa, 2018). As a research team, to varying degrees, we experience these same challenges and they are carefully interrogated in this chapter.

Scholarship lagged on the growth of a South African Black middle class after 1994. However, research on the Black middle class has been gaining momentum over the years with seminal manuscripts emerging within ten years (Alexander, Ceruti, Motseke, Phadi, & Wale, 2013; Khunou, 2015a; Krige, 2012; Phadi, 2010; Seekings, 2009; Southall, 2016). It is, therefore, the intention of this chapter to contribute to the growing body of research on the South African Black middle class and eventually to the study of the global Black middle class.

DISCUSSION OF FINDINGS

Perceptions and Preconceptions about the Black Middle Class

While some of the team members had preconceived notions that Blacks in the middle class were going to be pretentious, stuck-up and not welcoming of those not equal to their class status, other team members did not hold such preconceptions, especially none that centred on more negative views. These differences help us understand the insider/outsider dynamic and how othering occurs, and how to humanise how we "collect knowledge, classify and present it" (Smith, 2008). Leo came to the research project with a more open mind. He reflected that,

> *As a Nigerian [middle class man] living in South Africa, I did not have any preconceptions of the Black middle class that [were] based on my own personal experience of members of this class and felt no need to question their actions.*

Leo went on to say that he did not go into the interview questioning the actions and behaviours of members of the Black middle class before the interviews. This is usually associated with "insiderness", where one's positionality and the positionalities of one's inner circle are normalised. According to Smith (2008), insiderness demands more critical thinking as the consequences of one's findings have long-term personal costs, and thus demands constant reflexivity.

However, Leo's Nigerian heritage also makes him an "outsider" to some of the salient discourses of Blackness and middle classness in the South African context. Chigumadzi (2019) would explain this, in part, along the lines of an "experience gap" in Leo's lived reality as a Nigerian Black when juxtaposed against those of Black South Africans. Leo's so-called experience gap resulting from his outsider status as a Nigerian man does not necessarily mean he is not similarly implicated as insiders. Smith (2008) argues that thinking that outsiders are not involved is a result of limited positivistic attitudes to social research. It is, however, noteworthy that the evolution of class in Nigeria is not directly hinged on historical foundations of race relations or disparities; thus, there is a different formation of the middle class in this predominantly Black context (Chigumadzi, 2019). Hence, the dynamics associated with Blackness and middle classless are experienced very differently in Nigeria; this, then, makes for an interesting experience of the Black middle class in South Africa by Leo.

Leo goes on further to suggest that his economic background coupled with his educational pursuit of a PhD eased any apprehension he might have had with high profile respondents. Leo reflected that:

> *Perhaps, I was able to cover up for my lack of social capital with cultural capital in terms of education, and some access to economic capital (Bourdieu, 1986), and I think I drew a lot on this when engaging participants.*

The above reflection illustrates an involvement, where Leo was forced to think about his own positioning in comparison to the participants. When Leo says "I was able to cover up" in the above extract, it is clear that he is grappling with the dynamic of his outsider/insider status to middle classness, as he has some, but not all, of the elements that make one middle class. Leo reflected further that:

> *In hindsight, however, I think my positioning, and the sensibilities associated with it, had its positives as it made me engage the participants more robustly when my interviews with them [are] taken as a whole. I did not feel any real pressure to prove myself to anybody as far as the subject of class or middle classness is concerned, which helped me to have rich conversations with them.*

On the one hand, Leo indicates that he has the education, the original middle class family background, and what he refers to as some access to economic capital. On the other hand, he shows that he was not middle class in the same way as most of those he interviewed, with regards to access to a middle class occupation and income. This dilemma in Leo's reflection illustrates the fluctuating nature of the insider/outsider dynamic, and that one is never fully only one (Moore, 2015).

While Leo was confident about socialising with the Black middle class, three other team members, Lesego, Polite and Mabone, harboured negative and contested preconceptions of the Black middle class. Unlike Leo, Mabone, Polite and Lesego grew up working class, associate mainly with the working class and still live in predominantly working-class neighbourhoods in Soweto. For Mabone, who aligns himself more with the working class, his struggles were associated more with questions of the existence of a Black middle class demographic group instead of how the group may or may not behave. This was also true for Polite, who in her reflections argued; *"I did not believe there was a middle class, especially not a Black middle class"*.

Is it possible that the preconceived notions presented in Polite's and Mabone's case are a reflection of the view that well-off Blacks are not black enough and thus they cannot exist, or that if they exist they do not experience oppression resulting from how Blackness is conceived? This dilemma is influenced by apartheid's conception of Black as a monolithic group. Canham and Williams (2017) indicate that society tends to use narrow and limited definition of Blackness. These conceptions are based on assumption of absolute terms on Blackness, which excludes those who do not necessarily have the generalised "Black" identity in post-apartheid South Africa. Additionally, Khunou (2015a) illustrates how differentiation by class was challenging for Blacks during apartheid as middle classness for Blacks did not confer the same social mobility as it did for Whites. This is echoed in Alexander et al. (2013), in *Class in Soweto*, who show that in Soweto those who could easily identify as middle class occupy a precarious position and thus identify with the working class. Similarly, Krige (2015, p. 3), in *"Growing up" and "moving up": Metaphors that legitimise upward mobility*, notes that "mobility has become a metaphor for a range of transformations a younger generation of Africans have experienced". However, what emerges from Krige (2015) is how middle classness is deliberately used in contemporary South Africa to illustrate different types of mobilities including "physical mobilities and cultural crossings". This preconceived notion was shared by Lesego, as we will discuss shortly.

Another important discussion with regards to the existence of the Black middle class is the precarious nature of this class position for Blacks, given their lack of historical capital. Polite's contention is also focused more around sustainability of the position. This idea of precarity of the Black middle class is a growing critique in South African public discourse (Ndinga-Nyanga, 2019), and in academic literature (Ndletyana, 2014; Southall, 2016); and it is argued to have negative implications for maintaining democracy.

With Lesego, her previous experience with the behaviour of her wealthy uncle caused her to see the Black middle class as snobs, in part because of her uncle's residential choices. Lesego did not question the Black middle class existence but she questioned where they lived. She shared the following reflection:

> *When I embarked on the project of the global Black middle class, I had my own biases and preconceived notions already and I did not understand why we are interviewing people who live in wealthy suburban areas. Having to know where they reside was a problem for me, I mean most areas the interviews were conducted from, I had never been there, and it was for the first time I have been to those areas. During the interviews, I never used taxis or the Rea Vaya bus which are my primary modes of transport but for this project I had to use Uber, ask for lifts, and also was driven around by the African Pride hotel transport services. I felt like the areas were not accessible for me and this made me think that perhaps I was right about people who have money; that they tend to move to areas where public transport is not easily accessed and this meant that not everyone could come around and visit them. My uncle also stayed in one of the wealthy residential areas; he had a double-storied house but my extended family members who were from the township and had no car struggled to go and visit him. I constantly questioned their*

> *Blackness, I would overtly call the Black middle class snobs, coconuts and white imitators who think they are better than us. However, being part of this project, I was shocked because I got to understand that there is nothing better about the middle class; they are human beings like poor people, they just have more money than others. My mentality and perceptions started changing because most of the participants were kind and full of humility and that's one thing I had not expected from them.*

Lesego reflects on how her previous experiences with her uncle caused her apprehension because the Black middle class occupied residential areas that were historically assigned to Whites. She had reasons and past experiences to draw from that suggest the Black middle class will be unwelcoming of her and cause her to question her belonging in such spaces. From her perspective, and although they share the same skin colour, the class differences overshadow their racial similarities. Thus, she preemptively questions the Blackness of the Black middle class and the authenticity of their racial identity. The question that resonates in Lesego's mind is how some members of the Black middle class wilfully exclude a certain type of Black person who does not meet their understandings, perceptions and behaviours of middle classness. Also, Lesego's contestations show the continuous scrutiny by those who are not middle class. Many who are not middle class tend to be judgemental towards those who live in historically White suburbs, believing them to be problematic Blacks. Their move to historically White suburbs is problematised, their move is seen as lack of solidarity with Black politics. Thus, the assumption held is that they might forget their roots or they might forget the everyday struggles most people have in predominately Black townships or rural areas.

This reflection by Lesego resonates with the broader colonial and apartheid intentions for creating a Black middle class. Ndletyana (2014) illustrates that the intention was to divide and rule in order to build legitimacy for the apartheid state and do away with Black unity and radicalism among Blacks. This divisive strategy worked to some extent, as in the lifestyle and resource differentials experienced between *amakholwa* and *amogqoboka* (the civilised ones, who were mainly middle class) and the "resistant natives (known as *amaqaba* – illiterates)" (Ndletyana, 2014, p. 6).

In some circles, there is a tension that Blackness means having to struggle and is not equated with excellence, middle classness or even success. This tension caused Lesego to question the Blackness of this group while Mabone stressed his preconceived notion of the existence of a Black middle class in the following narrative:

> *Having been a working class black student in a tutor role, I assumed my experiences of race and being would be significantly different from those of the Black middle class. This position I had as "black, the real black" who fought and tried to change society, imagined the Black middle class as co-opted into white society. I prejudged them; it brought discomfort in the thought of interacting with them. I had imagined the participants to be 'Good Blacks' who lived and experienced the world as a colorless existence.*

Mabone assumed the Black middle class were devoid of substance. This notion reverberates in the earlier work of the American scholar, Frazier (1957, p. 195), that: "The black bourgeoisie suffers from "nothingness" because when [they] attain middle class status, their lives generally lose both content and significance". Mabone's initial perception of the Black Middle Class is described adequately by Canham and Williams (2017) as the Black gaze. The Black gaze "monitors the transgressions of class boundaries and establishment and accepted norms of black behaviour. It seeks uniformity and loyalty to black disadvantage or working-class identity" (Canham & Williams, 2017, p. 29). Mabone goes on to discuss his views following interaction with these "clever Blacks"– the term "clever Blacks" was first used by former president Jacob Zuma to reprimand those Blacks who were seemingly too smart for their traditions. According to Kitis, Milani, and Levon (2018), the term was then carried in a newspaper article titled *"Zuma scolds 'clever' blacks"*. Since then, the term became a metaphor to refer to class and race (Kitis et al., 2018). Reference to the Black middle class as "clever blacks" by then-President Jacob Zuma is in alignment with the earlier divisions mentioned by Ndletyana (2014).

However, once Mabone experienced these so-called "clever Blacks", he realised that, notwithstanding their successful lives, they still held strong Black racial identities. He acknowledges that, because of the interaction with the participants, he had changed his preconceived notion of the Black middle class. He reflected that:

> *I soon realized I was wrong and naive, they were really Black success ... they articulated experiences that were relatable to me, including the existential experiences of Blackness, I was shocked and taken aback. I felt like an insider to a domain I perceived myself an outsider [to] ... It was exhilarating to see and learn about their pride in their identity as both Black and middle class.*

Mabone's experience here illustrates how the idea of insider and outsider as stable and as a single position is not an accurate indication of how insiderness and outsiderness are experienced. Mabone illustrates the limitation of creating totality of identity. There is complexity in the intertwined roles and identities that people occupy in society. Beyond that, he acknowledges that one can experience comparable encounters to people they consider outside their lived reality. In recognising that the participants shared similar ideas about the global oppression of Black people, and the significance of emancipation, Mabone then reviewed his initial view of what it means to be a well-off Black, thus acknowledging that there are Blacks who are middle class, a position he initially refuted. Most importantly, however, is how Mabone acknowledges the shared experiences of oppression that Blacks generally experience as they navigate a continuing racialised world.

Like Mabone, Lesego also felt that the Black middle class would not have a strong racial identity and reflected in the following way:

> *I never thought they would be for Black solidarity and Black identity. I thought they would be more anti-Black and snobbish and only to find out they also had issues regarding racism and they wanted to belong. They questioned issues of hair and language. I felt guilty for always having to perceive them in a negative way.*

After contact with the participants, Lesego was able to question and thus shift her initial othering of the Black middle class, as she now saw her positioning as both an insider as a Black woman and an outsider only with regards to her class position. Lesego's change of heart in the above extract echoes Mabone's as they both come to acknowledge what Biko and Fanon mean when they talk about Black as a collective experience of oppression. This change of heart is eloquently described by Manganyi (1973) in *"Being Black in The World"*, which argues that the world is racialised and will continue to be so irrespective of your social status, class and stratification, your race continues to play a significant role in identity politics. Racial identity cannot be escaped and global and national racial subjugation is a lived reality for Black people.

For Polite, the shift in her initial ideas about the Black middle class was not a clear one. She reflected that given the precarious nature of Black middle class she still held that it was ...

> *... was more an experience than a position; most of them are unable to sustain the social and economic cushion provided by this class experience, thus it is not a position.*

Polite's dilemma on whether Blacks can be properly middle class is one held by a number of individuals and shared in literature by multiple scholars including Khunou (2015a), Krige (2012, 2015) and Southall (2016). Even though Polite's interaction during the field work involved older and younger women, she was mostly affected by, and reflects a lot more on, her experiences with the older women:

> *They strive for excellence in how they dealt with life; this convinced me of an existence of a middle, and maybe even a middle class ." If I had to define black middle class after my interviews with these women, I would say it is the excellence to strive to self-define. There's no middle in excellence and these women were black and excellent.*

Polite's reflection here speaks to the contestation around conceptions of the Black middle class and how middleness, as conceived in African languages, means being in the middle in very different ways to how middle classness is historically conceived in the social sciences (Phadi & Manda, 2010). Again, in Polite's case, we see her identification with the possibility of a middle class come up and resonate with her valuing of excellence that is shared by the older women she interviewed. Although she is still sceptical of their middle classness, there is an insider connection with their notion of excellence.

Again, even though Lesego and Mabone started with negative experiences about the Black middle class which initially affected how they contributed during the conceptualisation of the study, the development of the interview protocol and their earlier data collection. What, however, was interesting to observe is how, substantive contact with the Black middle class, as suggested by the intergroup contact hypothesis (Allport, Clark, & Pettigrew, 1954), reduced their levels of prejudice against the group and in some ways completely eliminated their negative perception. For example, Mabone reflects that:

> *The experiences that I had during the data collection had an impact on the ideas and notions I had on the Black middle class. The pre-conceived notions that I had about the Black middle class before I collected data have significantly changed.*

Mabone's reflections above echo feminist researchers; stance on reflexivity (Mama, 2005; Oakley, 1981). As indicated in the earlier chapters, we maintained constant reflection on our beliefs, positions and experiences throughout the research process; this might have forced not only Mabone but the entire research term to meditate deeply on the ideas we held and thus to be open to surprise as we engage with the research phenomenon and the participants.

Polite provided an interesting narrative that concluded with how she came to the project of studying the Black middle class with apprehension, in part based on her preconceived notions, and after she finished interviewing participants she had more questions than she had answers. Polite addresses this internal conflict in the following manner in her reflections:

> *Middle class for me represents opposite sides of socio-economic positionality that is compromised and is faced with complex debates, which still leave me with a lot of questions.*

On the one hand, initially, Polite was dismissive of the existence of the Black middle class. Although she continues to question the concept after her interaction with this cohort, she is no longer dismissive of their existence. On the other hand, while Mabone and Lesego started with more negative stereotypes about the Black middle class, Kris did not share the same stereotypes. Kris's encounter with the Black middle class was influenced by her scholarship in the American context where there is no official definition of middle class. The United States Census Bureau uses several measures related to income distribution and income inequality, but it does not have an official definition of what constitutes the American middle class. Thus, scholars have struggled for decades to decide who among the Black population should be considered middle class. W.E.B. Du Bois started this discussion in 1899, in his book *The Philadelphia Negro: A Social Study*, a sociological analysis of life among Blacks in an urban setting. St. Clair Drake and Horace R. Clayton (1945) continued subtly engaging this conversation in their book *Black Metropolis: A Study of Negro Life in a Northern City*. It was not until 1957, however, that a scholar dedicated an entire book to understanding every aspect of the Black middle class, analysing their attitudes, behaviours, beliefs and values. E. Franklin Frazier's (1957) seminal work *Black Bourgeoisie* was received with mixed reviews. According to the publisher's website, Simon & Shuster, the book was

> *simultaneously reviled and revered—revered for its skillful dissection of one of America's most complex communities, reviled for daring to cast a critical eye on a section of Black society that had achieved the trappings of the white, bourgeois ideal.*

Frazier developed, and his protégé Nathan Hare (1965) supported, a notion that the Black middle class lived in a "world of make-believe" and "conspicuous consumption", trying to emulate their White counterparts. While few scholars today would promote Frazier's and Hare's views.

Thirty years after the release of *Black Bourgeoisie*, Bart Landry (1987), published *The New Black Middle Class*. Both Frazier and Landry were looking specifically at the social structure as well as the behaviours, practices and decisions that caused this segment of Black America to be considered by themselves and others to be members of the Black middle class. Since Du Bois' (1899) seminal study in 1899, more than a dozen books have been written focusing on the Black middle class, but most of the scholarship has focused on the Black poor, or has approached the Black population in relation to national economics from a deficit model such *The Moynihan report* (Moynihan, 1965). The literature specific to the Black middle class, however, covers a wide array of topics including the depths and relentlessness of the everyday racism Blacks face (such as *Living with racism: The Black middle class experience* by Joe Feagin and Melvin Sikes (1994)); understanding how Black executives and professionals experience racism in the workplace (*Black corporate executives: The making and breaking of a Black middle class*, by Sharon

Collins (1997)) and in their neighbourhoods (*Black picket fences: privilege and peril among the Black middle class* by Mary Pattillo McCoy (1999, 2013)); how their spatial location can inform their social identities (*Blue-chip Black* by Karyn Lacy (2007)); the forces of institutionalised racism that continuously undermine their security (*The Black middle class: social mobility and vulnerability* by Benjamin Bowser (2007)); how they socialise their children to combat those forces (*Mothering while Black: boundaries and burdens of middle class Parenthood* by Dawn Dow (2019)); and the continuing struggle to define the Black middle class (*The new Black middle class in the twenty-first century* by Bart Landry (2018)). This list represents a very small portion of the scholarship dedicated to Black America in general during a roughly 110-year span of published scholarship.

Kris brought this knowledge with her but attempted to keep an open mind on how and who the Black middle class is in South Africa. Yet she did approach this project with some apprehension. Kris was concerned about how her American status was going to be perceived by the South Africans. She spoke about this throughout the research process and reflected on how she grappled with this notion in our final meeting. Kris noted:

> *So two things. One, I keep coming back to this notion about American privilege, 'cause I'm really grappling with that ... myself and whether or not I use it for evil or for good, and really try to work through that. But I think that I got access because of some of the American privilege. But I want to make sure that I do use it for good and not for evil. So if American privilege allowed me into a certain space that none of us would have normally been in, I was like, we should all be able to take advantage*

of that and the other part is that people are willing and want to mentor; they're always willing to give advice, and people have emailed you like, "your students ...", I'm still getting email saying "your students are great. Please have them follow-up. Please ..." - they're emailing me; they're texting me talking about how great you are. So I think it's up to you, but they're, they are extending themselves to you if you want to take advantage of that. I think that's part, part of the humility of this class that we're talking about. They're like, they don't mind sharing the information, sharing what they know.

This narrative from Kris highlights two important points. The first is that her status as an American was viewed positively. The Black middle class study participants embraced her as an American. Her status as an American, and presumably her status as a Fulbright, opened the door for opportunities to interview some solid members of the middle class and some who considered themselves "highly privileged". We use the word highly privileged here because one of the participants used the term to refer to himself when we asked him the question, "*Would you define yourself as middle class? Why or why not?*" during the interview process.

The second issue that Kris raises in her narrative is that the Black middle class participants were extremely fond of the research team, especially the students, and were willing to open up their personal and professional networks to the student researchers on the entire research team. This willingness to share their networks challenges some of the preconceived notions some of us had about this demographic group prior to starting the interviews.

Kris, in her closing thoughts about her research experience and her time in South Africa, reflected on her gratefulness to be on a research team that did not have similar views; just like everyone in the Black middle class, whether in South Africa, American or globally, they do not all share the same views. Kris said:

> *I think I'm the most grateful that I got the chance to meet everybody and work together with everybody, and I think we have a really unique demographic here. I think we can make a nice contribution to the literature [as a research team] because from what I understand, [Roger Southhall's], current work is like all of Soweto. We're looking at ... a broader extreme category on both ends. So, I'm so excited to have, the diversity within the Black middle class because you can no longer call the Black middle class, whether it's here or in Soweto, monolithic. There's a lot of variation and our research is willing to address that.*

From the above reflections and discussions, it is important to note that preconceived ideas of the study phenomenon, when reflected on deeply at multiple stages of the study, can yield important insights not only about the issue under examination but about the researchers as well.

CONCLUSION

What is clear from the discussion above is that the researchers' insiderness and outsiderness play an important part in impacting interviews with the Black middle class. The preconceived ideas, as discussed above illustrate how the team's individual subjectivities influenced their initial ideas and actions towards the participants and the project. The working-class positions of Mabone, Polite and Lesego influenced their preconceived ideas about the Black middle class, differently from Leo's middle class positioning. This is observable, for instance, in how ease of movement was facilitated by the fact that Leo drives his own car, among other middle class factors, which created an environment of comfort among the study participants.

The discussion above captures questions around the existence of the Black middle class and issues around the Blackness of the Black middle class; it illustrates how preconceived ideas were dealt with, and how, with contact, these ideas changed. What is worth noting is that encountering the Black middle class led to constant reflections by the team and important shifts away from uninformed bias towards an awareness of the existential realities of the members of the South African middle class. This shift is important as it allows the researcher to "hear and interpret the behaviour of others" (Fusch & Ness, 2015). This was mostly true for Mabone, Lesego and Polite, who illustrated how their narratives changed because of the interactions with the Black middle class respondents. Yet, in the chapter on a conceptual moving target, Leo also experienced an alteration in some biases he held about the Black middle class in South Africa, particularly his uncritical association of this demographic with indebtedness and conspicuous consumption. These shifts also illustrate how the outsider/insider dynamic is in flux, and how both manifest simultaneously. This is evident in Leo's case. To some degree, Leo remains an outsider with regards to the extent of his access to the middle class position, but he remains implicated as a researcher.

Preconceived ideas about social phenomena and about research participants are unavoidable; therefore reflexivity matters. Reflexivity matters especially because preconceived ideas might cloud judgement, lead to biases during social research and most importantly dehumanise the study participants. Reflections of such preconceived ideas are especially important in studies of contested and difficult-to-define concepts like the Black middle class. This chapter provided a reflection on our team's preconceived ideas about the study participants and shows that there are potential dangers when such preconceived notions are not critically reflected on. It also revealed that there are benefits in acknowledging the assumptions we hold about our research participants, reflecting on how they have impacted on our interaction with them, and what they mean for our findings. The chapter also argued that when unquestioned, preconceived ideas might constrain full engagement with research participants and restrain how researchers engross themselves in the interview process, thus limiting the type of data collected.

In conclusion, it is also important to note that an important factor in thinking about preconceived ideas is the insider/outsider dynamic and how it manifests simultaneously at times.

4

THANK YOU, BUT I GOT THIS: GENDER DYNAMICS BETWEEN RESEARCHERS AND THE BLACK MIDDLE CLASS

INTRODUCTION

As illustrated in the previous chapters, studies on the Black middle class have been on the increase since 1994. What is evident in most of the South African scholarship on the Black middle class is the paucity of gender analysis. For example in many of these studies, including Alexander, Ceruti, Motseke, Phadi, and Wale (2013) and Phadi and Ceruti (2011), the multiple meanings of class position, issues of affordability, unemployment and social location are detailed without providing a gender analysis of those experiences.

In earlier literature on class from elsewhere in the world (Bendix & Lipset, 1953), it has been illustrated that to understand class it is not only important to address questions of class structure and class mobility, but also to focus on power differentials in stratified societies. Feminist scholars clearly indicate how experiences of the world are gendered and further show that gender, as an experience, is located within cultural systems and therefore its history and articulations must be critically charted along with other aspects of social systems (Collins, 2000; hooks, 2000; Oyewumi, 1997). It is therefore a serious limitation to engage in class analysis without providing a gender lens.

In this chapter, we use the gender lens to examine how gender shapes data collection. Research fieldwork is very crucial because this is where the researcher scrutinises the life of the participants. During research fieldwork, gender has an influence on the research process as gender dynamics affect the research project. Järviluoma, Moisala, and Vilkko (2011) argue that the concept of gender norms, its values, and the manner in which preconceptions arise when people of different genders or the same gender meet, and how they interact with each other, has a valued impact on the micro and macro levels of people's lives. Therefore, feminist writers like Oakley (1981) argue that the gender of the interviewer matters and yields different findings. Therefore, during research gender should be taken seriously (Järviluoma et al., 2011).

A motivating factor for signifying gender in this chapter, and in our reflexivity and analysis, is because middle classness for Blacks is a precarious position (Khunou, 2015b; Southall, 2016); is difficult to define (Burger, McAravey, & Van der Berg, 2015; Canham & Williams, 2017); and because other identity signifiers are also important for fully explaining social experiences and meaning-making than class (Bettie, 2014; Gopalda, 2013). Gopalda (2013) also states that various identities matter, including age, gender, citizenship, education, ethnicity, income, sexual orientation, socio-economic status, immigration and others. Therefore, it is important to note that each identity provides a different privilege and marginalisation in different contexts. It is thus the contention of this chapter that, since gender does not act the same in all contexts (Oyewumi, 1997, 2002), gender, as a category for analysis, is significant for understanding how women and men of this class experience Black middle classness differently. Most importantly for this chapter is, therefore, the question of how the gender of the researcher and the participants shaped the research encounter.

Furthermore, we are interested in using gender as a category of reflexivity as it presents an opportunity to think about and comprehend the politics of "representation, power, knowledge production and constant negation of identity" (Ampofo, Beoku-Betts, & Osirim, 2008, p. 1). For some scholars such as Martin (2005), such reflexivity presents us with an opportunity to "catch gender in practice". This idea of catching gender in practice is premised on an understanding that the gender positioning that people occupy, and action that people engage in, is influenced by how gender is understood in a context (Martin, 2005; Oyewumi, 1997; Oyewumi, 2002). This exercise has been useful for us as researchers to think about not only how our study participants shared varied experiences and conceptions of Black middle classness but also how we might have gendered them in our encounters during interviews. The gendering that happens during interviewing is mainly as a result of ideas held by both the participants and the researchers. This process of gendering is shown in levels of comfort or discomfort experienced during interviews and in performing counter identities so as to be viewed in more positive ways. The discussion below will also show that this gendering is not only acted upon by the researchers but by the participants as well. Again, the reflexivity engaged in this chapter allowed us to think about how, in our engagement with the question of what it means to Black and middle class, we were not only influenced by our identification with the class position but also by our conscious and or unconscious identification with a particular gender.

DISCUSSION OF FINDINGS

Gender Matching Interviews and Challenges along the Way

In most research projects, especially sensitive studies, gender pairing is essential and has a strong influence on the research project (Sutter, Bosman, Kocher, & van Winden, 2009). This is particularly effective where the researcher aims to understand the gender power dynamics in the phenomenon being researched, and for credibility of the data (Jewkes et al., 2006). Even though this study is not defined as sensitive in the strictest sense – that is, the participants would not be generally defined as vulnerable and the research question was not necessarily going to elicit delicate information – we were interested in limiting research complications by opting for gender pairing interviewers with the participants. Research has illustrated that, where women interview men and vice versa, gendering tendencies complicate the research encounter and at times the findings (Jewkes et al., 2006; Khunou, n.d). Gendering occurs when during social interactions men and women's, "construct each other through gendering practices and the practicing of gender" (Martin, 2003). In an unpublished paper, Khunou (n.d) illustrates how interviewing men for her study on fatherhood as a young woman led to discomfort and shorter, less in-depth interviews than her interviews with women. She argues that these differences might have been a result of how she held back when interviewing men and how the men held back because she was a young, childless woman. Therefore, to avoid similar dynamics, we intended to gender match our participants with the researchers. She reflected that:

> *When we were doing the protocol for the interviews as the whole team, it was decided that the majority*

> *of the interviews will be gender paired, where male researchers will interview male participants and female researchers will interview female participants.*

As indicated in Chapter 1, Kris, who is from the USA and was less familiar with African names, did most of the recruiting of the participants. Therefore, to do this gender matching, the research team attempted to identify participants' genders through the participants' names; even though there was an assumption that most of us knew the meanings of the names and which gender they were assigned to, there was a limitation in our assumptions. Once participants were allocated to individual interviewers we found that, in some cases, participants' names were gender neutral (Petrovski, 2018), and thus some of the female participants were allocated male interviewers and vice versa. Lesego had the following to say on this dynamic, during our final reflexive meeting:

> *In most cases we used the participant's real names to guide us in determining their gender, as some referrals had not indicated the gender of the prospective participants. I therefore ended up interviewing three male participants for the project. However, when I thought about it when I got to the interviews, these male participants names were gender-neutral; they could be used for both male and females. Like my name Lesego is used by men and women.*

Such a scenario presents the researcher with the need to be mindful of diverse research contexts; in many African settings, names are often gender-neutral (Ndelu, 2017; Van Fleet & Atwater, 1997). However, the assumption we made early in the project was that the participants' names would allow us to easily identify whether the participant was male or female. However, as Lesego would discover, some of her participants were male. It is therefore important that on recruitment of participants, the record should not only include names and contact details but gender and other social markers (Van Fleet & Atwater, 1997).

The dynamics of the researcher interviewing a member of the opposite gender after this realisation become important for reflection. Even though the research leaders Professors Khunou and Marsh have interviewed both men and women before, the emerging researchers in the study had either interviewed only men or only women before. Therefore, their experience with interviewing members of different genders elicited feelings and experiences worth reflecting on here. As Lesego points out:

> *It was my first time interviewing men, I did not think I would have a problem because they are just participants and what I needed to do was to conduct the interview. I thought I could see beyond their gender.*

In as much as it was Lesego's first time interviewing male participants, she notes that she did not think she would encounter any difficulties because they are just participants. However, Lesego quickly realised that participants are more than respondents are; they are gendered individuals and come from diverse gendered backgrounds and contexts (Butler, 2009). The other reason Lesego might have thought that interviewing men will be just another experience is because, as Oakley (1981) shows, gender in critical research assumes detachment during the interview process. Again, what Lesego did not acknowledge at the time was the fact that she herself was gendered in how she encountered the world and thus she would not be able to interact with these men as "*just participants*".

The fact that Lesego was raised a girl in a gendered world meant that her interactions during the interview process would also be influenced by how she was taught to see and be in the world. Khunou (n.d, p. 2) asserts that "individuals' subjectivities play an important role in shaping the research process and therefore the type of data gathered". Consequently, reflexivity allows us to acknowledge that we are part of the social world that we are researching and we are co-creators of the knowledge we are creating (Manderson & Block, 2016). This does influence the interviewing process, how the researcher is positioned, and how participants carry themselves during the interviews. The research experience of interviewing the opposite gender was also true for Leo who was interviewing women for the first time on this project. His research interest had initially been on masculinities. He shared the following reflections about his experiences of the interviews:

> *For me, I shifted my eyes away when I was interviewing them [Women]. In addition, because we were seating so close, I do not know what that did to me. But when interviewing a man, I do not ask myself is it appropriate to stare in the eyes all the time.*

Leo interviewed three women and found that his experience was very different from his experience interviewing men. His extract above provides an interesting case on why gender pairing is recommended, and perhaps desirable, in gender-sensitive research. It is telling when he says "*I shifted my eyes away…. because we were [sitting] so close*" – this raises important questions about what is appropriate with regards to eye contact and closeness. Leo mentions that he never thinks about these issues when interacting with men. Again, the issue of eye contact and or shifting one's eyes while in a conversation has been an interesting topic of discussion since it also denotes cultural differences. Where, in some social context shifting one's gaze might be construed negatively (during counselling) and in other cultural contexts looking down or looking away denotes respect (when a Zulu bride speaks to her father in law), the issue of eye contact might be linked to appropriate gender relations (Mtshelwane, Nel & Brink, 2016). Therefore, in different social contexts, depending on what is culturally acceptable among the genders, averting one's gaze and not feeling comfortable sitting too close is part of what we do as gendered beings. According to Lucal (1999, p. 782), for social relations to be deemed successful, individuals need to "present, monitor, and interpret gender displays". It could be argued that what Lucal (1999) is suggesting captures what Leo was doing in the context explained in the above extract.

When Leo is asked to tell us about his interview with women and if he experienced any differences in terms of his previous experiences or current experiences with interviewing men, he responded with the following commentary:

> *At first, I felt a, a bit of nervousness. You know, I, I felt a little nervous ... So if I'm sitting with a man talking to him for the next two hours, I will stare him in the eyes, and you know there's this, um, I don't know how to put it, and then I find myself sometimes taking my eyes away when I'm speaking to the women (laughing) ... I shift my eyes away when I'm interviewing them. And because we are sitting so close, you know, for the interview ... With a man, I'm not asking myself is this appropriate to stare in the eyes all the time.*

While the research team erupts into genuine and some nervous laughter in the recording of this commentary, Mabone raises similar concerns to those that Leo expressed. As he continues to laugh, Mabone notes that "*I looked forward to interviewing the woman. I can look and they be staring into my eyes continuously (laughing)*". Leo is happy that Mabone shares similar sentiments and then feels comfortable talking more about the gender dynamics between interviewer and interviewee, and when he is interviewing a woman as a man, especially when her husband is present. Leo offered the following concerns he had when interviewing a young married couple (the only couple interview we conducted for the larger study). He reflected that:

> *No. Seriously, I, I struggle with that, especially with that young couple ... we were sitting on a couch. And so close. And then I have to sit there and just stare into the eyes. There was a, was a discomfort in that ... I must confess, I don't care what she is thinking, you know-I mean she's a married woman, and (laughing) ... so, so yes. It was, it was, it was, that was a little, um, I don't know (laughs) ... Discomforting (laughs). I could still ask and probe as much as I wanted, and um, but I think it's just the ... the physical that, um, is a difficult space as it were ... How to negotiate that space ... Sitting so close with a woman ... and I love doing that. I love staring people in their eyes when I speak to them, when I interview them.*

Leo also interviewed a female Professor, during which he also felt uncomfortable as, when talking to her, he was staring in her eyes. He mentioned that the Professor's husband was busy walking around during the interview, which might also indicate the discomfort of the husband, as his wife was being interviewed by another man in their home. Leo's desire to stare into the eyes of his respondents is challenged when that person is a woman. However, Fox (2009) argues that, keeping "eye contact" is one of the good skills in research, because if the researcher did not make any eye contact the respondent would be inhibited and less comfortable in engaging during the interview. However, the limitation with Fox (2009) is that in different cultural context eye contact might actually lead to discomfort and thus an awkward interview. During our final fieldwork meeting, Leo continued talking about staring:

> *I love doing that. But it was a little ... you know, I mean, you're sitting [with a] professor and trying to stare ... the husband is somewhere walking around, strutting around there (laughing), there but, anyways I, well I think it's, it's, it is been an eye-opener for me ... it was just, it was just beautiful ... But again, I think it overall is been an eye-opener as a researcher. I've never felt, I think in all my level of research, this is the best I, I've experienced so far. It's been beautiful.*

Extending gender pairing even to studies that might not be as sensitive, like general studies on the Black middle class, is also useful. However, one must also take into consideration the encouraging unanticipated consequences of Leo's experience in terms of the discomfort around engaging reflectively on what is appropriate behaviour when a man interviews women as opposed to when a man interviews a man. As Leo explains, it was an experience of "*awkwardness*", on the one hand. On the other hand, he points out that interviewing women was as discomforting as it was enriching because he also "*learnt something about the instability of my masculinity that day*". The important consideration of gender pairing in non-sensitive research, then, ought to be juxtaposed against the positive outcomes for the broader feminist project when male researchers seriously reflect on their gendered interactions with female research participants. Leo's reflections allow us to think about how non-gender sensitive research can make "visible the ordinariness and the routineness" of gendering and sexualising in interactions between female and or male researchers and participants" (Harries, 2016, p. 48). This will also allow for understanding and implementing the practice of males as researchers and interviewees not being merely conduits for oppressive discourses (Harries, 2016).

On another note, Moore (2015) indicates that gender pairing might have negative impacts on the interview as sometimes men refuse to open up to other men. Thus, gender pairing needs to be done with this dynamic in mind. Again, in Khunou (n.d), interviewing led to open sharing which confirms Moore's assertion, but at times the men she interviewed mistrusted her because of the theme of her study and how they were positioned in public discourse.

We would, however, caution that the positive outcomes for the broader feminist project resulting from our honesty and serious reflexivity in this project might not always be achieved in contexts where the men doing research with women are not inclined to the feminist project or where reflexivity is not taken seriously in their researcher endeavours. In such cases, gender pairing remains the best option as power dynamics in society remain heavily biased towards men. We make this point, however, with a clear understanding that no one method will be fit for all (Harries, 2016). Manderson and Block (2016, p. 1,318) note that:

> *different settings allow or inhibit the ability of the research participants to position each other in terms of class, social and personal differences, and commonalities, adding contextual and interpretive information to the interview.*

GENDER TALK AND THE INTERVIEW PROCESS

When we had our final research meeting before Kris left South Africa, the notion of gender parity in interviewing came up again. The first person to bring up the point was Leo:

> *I have never interviewed women before ... I had never in all my, in my research work, it has always been men because I'm very much interested in masculinity ... and I think ... my thinking that, you know, if we are going to affect any change, that's, that's where actually change will come.*

Leo is suggesting that, as a researcher, we have to come out of our comfort zones and this might include interviewing someone of a different gender than our own. As indicated earlier, Leo then went on to discuss that his research interests had focused on men, but he welcomed the idea of interviewing women, after some self-reflection. Rapoport and Rapoport (1976) have indicated that, in some cases, some female participants might be comfortable being interviewed by male researchers, and in the same way male participants would be comfortable being interviewed by female researchers; these scholars are arguing that there should be flexibility with regard to gender pairing in research. Leo stated that it was a normal everyday experience when he was interviewing men, which he is used to because his interests are in interviewing men. However, as mentioned already, Leo found it *"beautiful"* and a *"new experience"* interviewing women who are in the middle class position. He reflected further that:

> *These are women who are earning a lot of money. You know. One is a professor; so the other one is an accountant... it was a new experience ... It was*

> *just (laughs) it was just, I don't know (laughing).*
> *I think it was just beautiful.*

Although Leo saw the experience as beautiful, he still expressed some apprehension about interviewing women respondents and it seems that most of his concern rested with the notion of his body language. It is clear from the extract above that how Leo talks about this experience is also filled with discomfort which is off-set with laughter. The laughter is followed by the words "*I don't know*", which illustrates inability to articulate how he felt.

Mabone's discomfort was when a female participant he interviewed did not do a security check on him before he came for the interview. He reflected in the following way:

> *So you did not verify how I look. You just take*
> *and you know. She mentioned once her house was*
> *glass. But it was like so you, there is no verification*
> *(laughing) and yet I am here and I say I am here*
> *to interview you and bam, I might be somebody*
> *else ... because somebody said I am a professor and*
> *I'm doing a study. I'm bringing someone who isn't*
> *me, who is a student and you don't do a count and*
> *check on me. You live in this house that is very fancy*
> *and so nice and you don't ask for ID. I'm like ... a*
> *lot of things just rip my mind cause the first thing I*
> *thought, she is a woman, and about safety, and I've*
> *only interviewed men. So with men, my safety was,*
> *my safety ... . But in one case, I asked like, this is*
> *so naïve of both of us, but more so for you because*
> *you know, you've only met Kris once. And then you*
> *allowing me into your space in this lovely home. And*
> *you have been no security check at all about who I*
> *am; you just taking my word for it.*

The burning question here is that if this was a male participant, would this have bothered Mabone? Why is Mabone trying to trap this woman into a victim existence? Is she not allowed to engage in the world like a human? Mabone genders this participant because she allowed him into her house without question in a country where reports of women's violation are a daily occurrence. Mabone genders this experience because the participant trusted the study leader who approached her, and she could not have thought of anything sinister that could have happened. But what Mabone is raising is something in research we could think about in how we should ensure the safety of participants, especially in cases where different genders are involved in the interview process (Rapoport & Rapoport, 1976).

When we discussed the women researchers interviewing the men, a slightly different but relevant perspective emerged. We turn to the dialogue by Lesego. At the last meeting we had, she shared:

> *It was, it was ... 'cause I've always [been] exposed to women in Grace's projects and stats. And my own dissertation. With men, it was, this was the first time I interviewed men. How do we, how do I sit? Do I look ... say there? 'cause ... like okay he's staring ... Okay, now these are men. Some are older; some are younger, but I have that respect for them as men. ... I was, was talking about this, um, the, the restaurant owner, he's fairly young. He looks young; he's a biker and he's really young and was giving me the eye. I was like (laughing). He's like, ah, come back after your interview (laughing), and he saying this in the interview and I'm like, okay. He kept staring and I ended up writing notes to avoid his stare. However with the other male*

> *participants who were married, I did not experience this and maybe because they were married.*

Lesego found it difficult interviewing men in the project, as she speaks about the aspect of body language, as she kept on asking herself which is the appropriate way to sit when interviewing a man. The respect that Lesego performed during the interviews was because of traditional gender dynamics; she felt there was a certain way she was expected to behave, to behave more like a woman and be respectful towards these male participants (Mtshelwane et al., 2016). On the one hand, this is a socialisation, which women carry out, as they are regarded as submissive, docile and respectful beings, especially towards men (hooks, 2000; Mtshelwane et al., 2016). On the other hand, when one of the participants made her uncomfortable as he continuously stared at her, she ended up writing her notes to self-distract and also to distract the participant from staring (Fox, 2009).

One of the things we picked in our analysis of how we talked about the discomfort that came up during interactions with the opposite gender is the use of laughter to ease the discomfort felt in sharing the uneasiness experienced during the actual interviews. According to Gronnerod (2004), even though laugher is not usually engaged with in social research it is an important analytical tool for understanding how data emerged and individuals manage how they are perceived by those they are interacting with. We see the use of laughter by Mabone, Leo and Lesego when sharing their reflections with the group on issues of sexualisation and gendering. Gronnerod (2004) illustrates that laughter is also used to negotiate heterosexual tensions. In the context of the reflection, these tensions were negotiated between the team but in retrospect with how they actually felt heterosexual tensions in the context of the actual interviews.

GENDER AND SEXUALISATION DURING THE INTERVIEW PROCESS

Another significant issue that arose with regards to interviewing members of the opposite gender was sexualisation. Järviluoma et al. (2011) argue that sexual politics in fieldwork are most common, especially when the genders of the interviewer and interviewee are different. People often act with their bodies before they can speak during interviews. Most female researchers have indicated that when they interview men, frequently they become uncomfortable as male participants would make advances on them (Järviluoma et al., 2011; Khunou, n.d.; Rapoport & Rapoport, 1976; Sutter et al., 2009). Similarly, Lesego was uncomfortable with the male participant who made sexual overtures during the interview and this could have affected the quality of the interviews she conducted with them. She reflected that;

> *One of the participants made me uncomfortable because he was 'eyeing me out' and plus how I was dressed made it worse for me. The other male participants, they were married and had children. Before, during and after the interview they made reference to their family as compared to the other male participant who was single.*

Because we are part of the world we are investigating (Manderson & Block, 2016), and trying to influence it positively, it is important that we recognise that in our attempts to do so during research, we engage with this world as well. On the one hand, Harries (2016, p. 48) argues that "… interview relationships mimic normalised gendered relationships and reflect the 'accepted' status of women researchers"; however, in Lesego's case, the discomfort was a result of the fact that the other male participants did not make similar advances, and diffused her discomfort by making reference to their children and wives during the interview. However, with the participant who made sexual advances on her, talk of significant others was not part of how he represented himself.

On the other hand, even though Grace and Kris did not directly speak about being sexualised during the interview, they note as experienced researchers that experiencing discomfort during interviews is also an indication of existing power dynamics. For example, Grace and Kris note that, power imbalance happen at times because of sexual advances as in Lesego's case, or because of cultural differences such as, in Leo's case, where looking men in the eye is affirming but uncomfortable if it is with a strange woman in a context of a research interview. Again, even though such discomfort would be highly expected in men, the above experiences show that women as well may feel uncomfortable because of a man's presence and because of the stature of the man.

Another point worth discussing is how the two male participants did not share any experiences of being sexualised by the women participants they interviewed. This indicates the inequality in social research with particular to how women researchers are positioned and how therefore their studies are impacted differently by gendered power dynamics. It is, however, worth noting that in sharing their discomforts Mabone and Leo are in turn indicating their vulnerabilities as men forced to "check themselves" so as to ensure that they are not crossing socio-cultural boundaries when interacting with women during research. Leo mentions earlier that he struggled with the question of what was appropriate, this questioning happens in context where feminism is gaining ground and where campaigns such as the #MeToo movement have pushed men to be reflective of their interaction with women and how they position women generally.

GENDER AND LENGTH OF INTERVIEW

Gendered socialisation has been argued to play a role in how women and men talk, especially how much they share during research interviews (Khunou, n.d). As a result, interviews with women are more nuanced because they share their experiences with others to have a favourable outcome in their goals. Whereas, those with men are usually shorter as men are seemingly less inclined to share.

Therefore, it might have been easier for women to draw from multiple narratives with other women to centre their stories of being Black, middle class and women. Our abilities as researchers to recognise, unpack and reflect upon our differences and relatability with participants bring rich and complex dynamics in the researcher–participant relationship, whether the research is set in mixed-sex paired interviews or in same-sex paired interviews. Polite believed that gender and length of interview matters especially when doing reflexive work with the participant. Polite reflected on her interview experiences:

> *When I was interviewing older women I would draw on the generational gaps of thinking to get the women to remember being young and their journeys throughout their lives; I learnt this when I interviewing men for my honours and master's degree; where I would say as "a girl I do not understand 1...2...3" and "help me understand 1...2...3. It was easier to draw out differences when it was men and women. My previous interviews with men were shorter despite my attempts to probe. This was my first time interviewing women in my research career, and based on gender- pairing advantage assumption is that relatability is obvious, but I did find myself questioning myself, "how do I relate to a CEO when I am merely a researcher.*

In the quote above, Polite raises an important aspect that although gendering pairing has its advantages it does not mitigate other issues of relatable that might come, like when Polite had to interview a woman CEO. She felt she was not equipped. Polite had no matching experience. However, on reflection Polite now realises that comparatively her earlier interviews with men in her honours and MA research project were shorter as compared to her interviews with women for this project.

It is often the case that male participants' interviews are shorter than those of the female participants. In an unpublished manuscript on interviewing men and women, Khunou (n.d) indicates how her gender led to different experiences with women and men who participated in her study in terms of length of the interview and the quality of the conversation with the men compared to those with the women. Lesego experienced the same thing, and she reflected in this way on her experience:

The three [male] interviews lasted long but not as compared to female participants, less than an hour or forty five minutes maximum. Female participants have a lot to say and they explain more as compared to male participants, male participants were more direct when asked questions and this made it difficult to even probe further.

Sometimes it is difficult for men to speak about their personal experiences and this is linked to how men have been socialised, as they are taught that, they are not emotional beings and should be less expressive than women (Petrovski, 2018; Sutter et al., 2009). What Lesego does not mention in the above extract is how the length of her interviews with men might have been influenced by her discomfort.

Another reason women get more detailed responses from interviewing other women is because the gender matching allows for a more relaxed interview process. Khunou (n.d, p. 21) illustrates that interviews between women tend to lead to "trust and assumptions of understanding by the woman researcher".

THANK YOU, BUT I GOT THIS: PERFORMING GENDER TO SHIFT STEREOTYPES

Although gender dynamics are usually considered significant in research between women and men, in Polite's experience it was important for her to position herself in contrast to older and more accomplished women (Ibanga, 2007). Her experience raises important considerations about gender, age and class position. Therefore, the phrase *"thank you but I got this"* denotes a move away from being defined as poor to a situation where one is seen as able to pay their own way. For Polite, performing the position of a girl who does not need to be taken care of was to shake off the stereotype that young women from Soweto were not hardworking and needed someone to pay for them (Mtshelwane et al., 2016). Research finds that in patriarchal contexts, older women usually play the role of policing younger women to behave as "proper" girls. In a context of class, then, middle class women tend to perform this task in relation to lower class women (Adichie, 2017; Sarkisian & Gerstel, 2006). Sarkisian and Gerstel (2006) illustrate that class differences are also experienced in gendered ways. Polite's experience below is her reflection on how she repositioned herself in her interaction with her women participants:

> *And the sense of pride from being a Sowetan girl came much into presence in refusal of pleasantries such as coffee, food, and if we were meeting at a public place, I would insist on paying my own bill.*

> *Although the participants offered the pleasantries as common courtesy or [on] the impression that I was a student or a field work researcher and therefore, they had a better economic standing to pay or offer the pleasantries; the pride that comes from ... being from Soweto would not allow me. Again my performance of gendered resistance against the backdrop of discourse that people from Soweto or those who do not occupy the Sandton spaces are always in need of some kind of help. Therefore, by simply refusing food or drinks even when I was hungry and thirsty, was my own way to show or display that their middle classness will not define parts of me in this process.*

It is usually assumed that women get each other. However, class plays a role in how women from different class and generational backgrounds see and view each other. So, the fieldwork process provides Polite the space to reconstruct what she viewed as erroneous public discourse on what it means to be a young woman from Soweto. By refusing to be provided a drink or a meal she affirms herself as not different from the older more established women she interviewed; she reconstructs herself, and maybe their story of her and generally the young Black woman from Soweto.

With the growing presence of the Black middle class, and more legal and political stances seeking to empower more social categories such as Blacks, women, youth and so on, there has also been a backlash in the misrecognition of what transformation of a Black young woman in South Africa looks like (Martin, 2005). One of the ways in which this was illustrated was the fear that Polite experienced when hearing that her generation was "lazy" because of the new freedoms that were earned in which women are no longer invisible. She reflects thus to how this fear influenced her interaction with her participants:

> *One of the participants, who had also explained that her mother was part of the study, narrated about being Black, female and young in a way that places questions around how people see women in the Black middle class and women in the working class. The participant went on to explain how she felt that she was not seen as a hard working woman by relatives because her family had a helper, and she could not escape the elder women's gaze from her relatives because of mother's facilitation of narrative in confirming the story of her 'laziness'. This experience was something I could identify with, the notion that educated girls that are not simply identifiable as working class are seen as lazy because they lack the 'labourious' or domesticated gene. Therefore, I was now beginning to understand that class was not only about socio-economic standings, but was also measured in performing certain gender roles that were seen as associated with women from a particular class.*

Given the existence of these public discourses, it was imperative for Polite to perform the opposite of how she felt she was being portrayed as a young educated Black woman who did not have to perform the normative roles associated with young Black women. Another reason Polite felt compelled to perform the strong identity of a young Black woman was that even though she interviewed women of multiple ages, she experienced most of them as still having the need to perform domestic chores (Adichie, 2017; Jones, 2010). What was a challenge for her was that this identification with "traditional" gender roles was also coupled with a need for and an aspiration for education as it was seen as emancipatory. She reflected that:

> *If there is one thing that I have taken from this journey [it] is that the middle class shows the brighter future if affirmative action were to be implemented from a bottom-up approach. Coming into this project, I had heard of the words such as Black girl magic and Black diamonds, and I received them skeptically. Nevertheless, being in the presence of successful Black women brought them into life. I realized that the words were as important as the people that represent them. Hearing of their daily struggles with a system that seemed to suffocate them and yet seeing them succeed made it all magic. It was not so much the term middle class that mattered but what their rise to success and their ability to rewrite the meaning of being Black and women in South Africa, one cannot separate the meanings of being in both these worlds without looking at the structures that shape the phenomenon of what it means to be "Black" and "women", when thought about separately and then together.*

On the one hand, unlike Polite's earlier assumptions that these women were not to be trusted with her vulnerability as a young Black woman from Soweto who had been defined as lazy, in the above extract it is clear that she also felt empowered by these women. It is also obvious she feels she identifies with them as well. On the other hand, Lesego did not initially show a need for a similar gendered resistance that Polite illustrated in her first encounter with her woman interviewees.

She felt that interviewing other Black women who were middle class was empowering for her. She reflected:

> *Interviewing women who are Black middle class was beneficial for me as a young Black woman, who is emerging because they served as an inspiration for me in achieving more. It is always important to look up to your own, people you are able to identify with.*

The journey for some Black women represented something powerful that symbolised what it might have meant to be Black and middle class in the apartheid days (Southall, 2016). Even though Polite found some resonance with these women, she still felt that they need to shift their perception of themselves somewhat. Polite reflected this by reflecting that:

> *These women were ambitious, focused, driven - yet it also meant not to forget your place as recognized in the world. All of which derives from the subpositions of being Black and female. Being a woman in their respective corporate positions in most cases meant they have to fight for recognition, had to be more assertive, and look at their journey in comparison to their White female, Black male and their White male colleagues. The many obstacles that they had to face in their professional lives, such as being second guessed [and] overlooked and the double labour contribution, is something Black women are always reminded of.*

This recognition of the multiple burdens of being Black and women increased the pressure for Polite to perform the strong gender identity. She felt the need at times to perform the smart young Black woman who asked interesting questions; was knowledgeable about current politics; and who had answers to every question. For Polite, this type of performance would allow her to intentionally change the stereotype that young Black women from the township carried. This research process allowed for self-reflection and intentional work to shift the narrative about young Black women from the township. According to Martin (2005), Polite used this research process to be reflective and to intentionally practice a particular gender. She further reflected that:

> *As a Black girl from Soweto, interviewing Black women from different contexts from [me] and some from the same township revealed certain dynamics of hidden and complex intersecting powers that shaped some of my interactions with the participants. Growing up I was taught a silent notion of mistrusting information or knowledge that is given by Black girls.*

As mentioned by Gqola (2017), Polite felt that she had the responsibility to listen to and recognise the knowledge shared by the participants as their knowledge and lived experiences. Therefore, as Polite acknowledged the identities of the women she interviewed and her intentional identity as a young Black woman with power to define herself, she felt some power, even though it did not feel constant. On the other hand, Lesego felt disempowered when one of her participants tried to take away from her the power she thought she had. Her reflection indicated the following:

> *One of the female participants was a bit [stand] offish towards me. I felt like I intimidated her as she kept on making comments off record, like she does not think being too educated is good enough and devalued my qualification. I felt it was unnecessary,*

> *but I understood how we as women are socialised to police each other and how we are made to compete against each other, while it's not necessary at all.*

This reflection is important as the backdrop of Polite's stance of performing the strong young Black woman. How could Lesego's feeling that she was being put down for being too educated take away from her the same ability to perform the stance of a powerful young Black woman from the township? Again, this extract illustrate a contradiction: earlier Lesego argued that interviewing Black middle class participants was beneficial for her. What the contrasting experiences illustrate is that a single way of responding to or performing an intentional gender script might not work in all instances and thus the interviewer is constantly challenged to read, reread and perform an appropriate intentional gender with different participants (Reid, Brown, Smith, Cope, & Jamieson, 2018).

CONCLUSION

This chapter illustrated the significance of gender analysis in reflexivity for studies on the Black middle class. Through the use of gender as a lens for collecting data, the researchers showed how various gender dynamics manifest in the field. Their discomforts in interviewing participants of a different gender indicates the significant role of gender pairing, as it makes it easier for both the researcher and the participant to engage comfortably with each other. However, the research team had to learn the skill of being flexible researchers in cases where they interviewed participants of different genders to theirs. It is therefore important to allow for non-gendered paired interviews when studies are not sensitive as this has the potential of allowing further reflexivity and new ways of engaging during such studies.

In conclusion, it is important to recognise that, given the fact that research about the Black middle class is fairly new and on the rise in South Africa, it is important to encourage further reflexivity as this will be useful for reimagining research methods, so as to humanise those we produce knowledge with.

5

WHAT DO I WEAR, AND DO I EAT THEIR FOOD? PERFORMING MIDDLE CLASSNESS

INTRODUCTION

Studies of class and social stratification have been useful in facilitating our understanding of how inequality manifests. Most of these studies have, however, focused on how inequality is expressed or experienced from the perspective of gender, race and region. Again, as indicated in the earlier chapters, Black middle class studies in South Africa have focused mainly on income, occupation and education, while less attention has been given to subjective measures in the research process. This chapter focuses on this latter theme in terms of the impact of physical appearance, dress and other personal matters of the interview process.

In the *Power of looks: social stratification of physical appearance*, Berry (2016) argues that, individuals who do not display the finest outfits, or those whose appearance does not fit the norm, experience prejudice and discrimination. She further asserts that looks matter because "we gain and lose social power depending on our physical appearance" (Berry, 2016, p. 12). In addition, dress has been defined as a collection of adjustments used to "communicate and enact various identities" (Johnson, Lennon, & Rudd, 2014; Kang, Sklar, & Johnson, 2011). Thus, how one is dressed is an attempt at constructing and communicating a certain self-identity. Together with this, one's actions in social settings, including decisions regarding accepting food, a ride or other "favors", is influenced by the individual's assumptions, beliefs, perceptions and feelings about themselves and those they are interacting with (Johnson et al., 2014). This chapter will, therefore, show how team members manoeuvred around such subjective measures during interviews with participants, particularly how decisions around dress, food and transport were negotiated. It will also reveal the relevance of gender in this process, and the discomforts experienced since women's and men's encounters during interviews are different.

Even though early methodology textbooks prescribed that researchers are expected to be mere observers during interviews, this is not entirely true because researchers also "act" during the interview process (Mama, 2005). Researcher characteristics such as age, race, ethnic group, class and gender have an impact on how the researcher appears in the research process, and that in turn influences the researcher's interaction with the participants. Lisiak (2015) suggests that researchers are active participants in interviews as they bring in props, which assist them in performing their position as researchers. Tools that allow researchers to perform the researcher position include the voice recorder, notepads, cameras and interview guides, among others. The use of these tools and the label of researcher indicates that researchers pose a different embodiment during interviews, and this is evident in the way they talk, dress and it is also true in their body language (Lisiak, 2015). This performance of the researcher position creates an impression of who they are (Lisiak, 2015). Thus, the idea that "the interview is an embodied experience" is confirmed (Manderson & Block, 2016).

Again, it is very common that researchers have perceptions about their research participants. Although having preconceived assumptions about the study participants and the phenomena under investigation is inevitable, it is important to note that when these pre-conceived ideas are not critically engaged with, they create challenges in the interview process. Lisiak (2015) argues that having assumptions as a researcher is essential; however, assumptions that are created should not be reducible to the participant because the assumptions the researcher might have about the respondent might not be true. This chapter engages with how the preconceived ideas we held about the participants influenced how we presented ourselves in terms of dress and acceptance of food or drinks. Our class performance was heightened as a result of these assumptions.

DISCUSSION OF FINDINGS

Performing Middle Classness – When How We Look Matters

The influence of how researchers dress and how they carry themselves is hardly documented in literature focusing on research methodologies. However, it is important to note that how researchers appear in front of their participants influences the research process as most researchers do believe in the phrase "first impressions matter" (Carling, Bivand, Erdal, & Ezzati, 2014; Goffman, 1959) and dress plays an important role in this.

In South African townships, fashion and clothing are amongst the markers that individuals use to perform social status and belonging to a particular social stratum. Leopeng and Langa (2019) highlight this significance in their analysis of a popular men's magazine and illustrate that fashion and consumerism is signified in conceptions of contemporary middle class masculinities. Canham and Williams (2017) highlight that the expression of Blackness and Whiteness are constituted through performativity, which Butler (2009) suggests is acquired through the ability to appear "natural" or present a social action repetitively. However, performance of social action is not stable because of the various audiences that must "buy into" the performance and further ensure that it must have a social consequence. So, to dress up in a particular manner is not a simple act of avoiding committing the social taboo of nakedness. Fashion or dressing up politically conveys assumptions about class, race, gender, age and so on. This is important as Polite reflects on how she performed her assumptions about these social factors during the interviews:

> *By dressing in a certain way, I wished not to be a reminder of where I possibly come from, I wished to reflect their progress and achievement, to go beyond the expected. To dress in a certain way, for me, meant I did not want to be a stereotype that Blacks could not be progressive. I did not want to wear a Converse sneaker as a young woman from the township in the participants' homes or workplaces because where I come from, township girls that wear converse sneakers are considered 'clevers'/streetwise, and you cannot bring that into someone's place of respect and progression.*

By adhering to what, in Polite's knowledge, was the norm meant that she could protect herself from being labelled a streetwise young woman from the townships. She wanted to fit in, to belong in a way the participants would find "acceptable" and, therefore, she assumed that how she dressed would help her achieve this. Berry (2016) asserts that, given that women know the costs of non-compliance, it is strategic for them to play the game so that they do not continue to pay the cost. Even though this is too much work for women, it is important to acknowledge that when they do not comply, they pay dearly. Similarly, Lesego also wanted to fit in with her participants, although, for her, the issue was not about how township girls are seen as streetwise but more to hide a working-class background. She dressed in such a way as to affirm her middle classness as an interviewer. Lesego reflected in the following way to show how she performed middle classness during the interviews:

> *I come from a working-class background. I do not own expensive clothes but for the interviews I wore clothes I normally wear to church or on special occasions. I always believed first impressions last and matter.*

In most Black poor or working-class societies, it has long been the case that formal or one's best clothes would be worn on special occasions such as going to church, weddings, funerals and other special occasions and this was because they could not afford to buy expensive clothes to be worn every day. For Lesego, then, having to dress up for the interviews meant she treated the interviews like the special occasions she attends, and this meant she was performing to fit in with her perception of what it means to be middle class (Goffman, 1959). She did this so as to impress her middle class participants. Lesego's interpretation of the link between dress and class is spot-on. Research illustrates how to dress during apartheid was used to determine social position and thus to create Whiteness as superior (Nuttal, 2004; Posel, 2010).

There is a long history between dress and social positioning; in early society, dress was used to distinguish between the upper classes and the lower (Blumer, 1969).

Human beings care what other people think of them and how they are dressed can mask the deficiencies that individuals have concerning how they are perceived in particular social contexts. This need to fit in influenced Lesego's actions and her reflection on how she was performing middle classness:

> *I wore my best clothes and I did this because*
> *I wanted to look representable and feel good*
> *about myself. I felt good though in how I looked.*
> *I wanted the participants not to undermine me*
> *and think I am not middle class, or I am not*
> *good enough for their time; thus, I had to always*
> *emphasize how educated I am before the interview*
> *commenced. I did not want to be seen as the*
> *student but as someone capable of conducting an*
> *interview.*

Lesego cared about how participants would view her. She felt that because they are middle class, if she came to the interviews wearing her everyday casual clothes, they would have not approved of her. In the above extract, Lesego uses the words "*not good enough*" to illustrate how respectability and acceptance are linked to how one looks and or what one is wearing (Blumer, 1969). She made sure that she wore her best clothes so they could identify with her and so she could also fit in. This idea of respectability, and its links to how one looks, is an old idea in stratified societies where clothing is used as a symbol of status and differentiation between different social classes. Adam and Galinsky (2012) argue that how people dress, in most cases, affects their cognitive process as they look at themselves through others' eyes, and this brings them affirmation of themselves. Adam and Galinsky's (2012) argument echoes Lesego's view that her Sunday best clothes made her feel good and thus look the part.

The understanding of Sunday best clothing supports the notion of politics of respectability. Black people began to embody something called respectability politics or the politics of respectability through dress and other everyday social ways of being and interacting. In essence, the term suggests that marginalised people (in this case, Black people) police, scrutinise, and correct their actions and the actions of members of their own groups so that they represent the group they belong to, or the group they aspire to belong to, with social values and norms commensurate with dominant values and mores. For example, members of the Black middle class would prescribe for themselves, other members of that class, and members of the working classes how to comport one's self in public, how to dress, speak and act to emulate the behaviour and social norms of the White middle class.

The politics of respectability as a term first rose to national attention in the United States in Evelyn Brooks Higginbotham's (1993) book, *Righteous discontent*. In it, she addresses the role of Black women in the Black church and how they challenged racism and sexism while demanding various equal rights, employment and opportunities for women through a "politics of respectability" lens of good manners and exemplary deportment respected and valued by the larger society. In South Africa, these politics of respectability are captured in Ndletyana (2014) in his discussion of how the African middle classes, during colonisation and apartheid, used dress and the English language to fit in. The critique of respectability politics is that it does not allow Blacks to have preferences, tastes and demeanours that are not palatable to the larger community. Furthermore, it tells Blacks to fit in instead of challenging the failure of the dominant discourse to be more accepting and inclusive of other cultures.

Additionally, one notices how Lesego intersected dress and her education to gain acknowledgement from those she interviewed. She constantly had to affirm herself by always informing the participants how educated she was. Education is one of the objective measures of middle class status (Ndletyana, 2014; Southall, 2016). It is worth noting that using education as a marker of middle class status was discussed in other chapters and used as an additional performance tool for members of the research team. Lesego might have been more educated than some of the participants she interviewed, and this is one of the attributes that made her feel good and above some participants who had not acquired a master's degree. Her education was used to mask the deficiency she had with regards to the class position. Berry (2016) contends that even though it should not matter how we look, nor, in our opinion, how educated you are, we have found that, irrespective of what we think and what Berry suggests, it does matter. The fact that it matters in a socio-economic context marred by inequality means that our choice to look as we please and acquire whatever education we want is limited.

In Chapter 4 we indicated that gender pairing in research is essential because most participants become comfortable when being interviewed by someone of the same sex. We also illustrated that even though we used gender pairing as a strategy because of gender-neutral names, some of the team members were shocked to find that the people they were allocated to interview were actually of the opposite sex. This was true for Lesego, who ended up interviewing three male participants. For one of these interviews, Lesego felt uncomfortable having to interview the young man because of how she was dressed. She shared that:

> *I was coming from a tombstone unveiling ceremony and was called to conduct an interview as the*

> *participant was only available at that time. I was wearing a tight body-con dress, heels and a long coat. I did not think I was interviewing a male participant until I got to the research site and I felt completely overdressed and uncomfortable because the participant also made a move on me.*

The discomfort Lesego felt was because she deemed her dress code was inappropriate for interviewing a man. To make matters worse, the participant made a move on Lesego and she felt it was because of the fitted short dress she was wearing, which appeared to suggest she was giving something off (Goffman, 1956). Lisiak (2015) in her study shows how difficult dressing up can be for a female researcher because how women dress is constantly scrutinised and the perception is that they dressed to please men, be it in a professional or non-professional space (Adam & Galinsky, 2012). In this case, Lesego dressed innocently for a personal occasion she was attending and came to the interview dressed the same way as she was not aware she was going to be conducting an interview that day. However, there was discomfort for her in how she was dressed. Her appearance made her feel out of place and the reaction of the male participant to her contributed to her feeling that how she looked was not appropriate. It is clear from this example that even though it should not matter how we look as argued by Berry (2016), it does matter in contexts where one will either be denied access or will receive unwelcome attention as in Lesego's case. Berry (2016) also offers that the challenge with gender, dress and discrimination is that at times women do not have a choice, as their choice, as in Lesego's case above, is influenced by cultural limitations.

Another important issue to note in the above quote is that Lesego says that she did not dress for the interview; this indicates that dress in her everyday life plays a different role than it does in other aspects of her life. In terms of the study and fieldwork, the preconceived ideas the team members had and Lesego had about the middle class participants influenced her ideas on how she needs to represent herself. She said:

> *I have always had a perception about the middle class; that they dress in a particular way, eat particular food and speak in a particular way. Thus, I observed everything about them. During the interviews, I noticed how they always wore formal and smart-casual clothes. Some participants would be wearing formal clothing, like a formal shirt, skirt, trousers, and formal shoes during the interview. There were those participants who wore ordinary clothes similar to the ones I wear at home or when I am on campus.*

It is essential that when a researcher enters the field, she is aware that participants will assume and portray different identities. However, it is important to know that these perceptions might not be true for every participant. Generally, Lesego had various perceptions when it comes to middle class people, about how they dress and carry themselves. Lesego felt that her participants were performing middle classness in the way they were dressed as they wore formal and smart-casual clothes. One reason for this could be that some of the interviews took place at the participants' workplaces, thus the formal dress. Yet some interviews were conducted in the evening, in public places or participants' homes, and many participants were still wearing formal clothes as they came to interviews either straight after work and or other engagements that require formal dress. Even though there are work-related reasons for dressing in a way that makes people look good, Berry (2016) asserts that the reason why we do it is also because, when we do not, the punishment that is dispensed out might be too costly, including losing your job and or losing social access to opportunities. Furthermore, Leopeng and Langa (2019) illustrate that dress, fashion and even hairstyles can be a marker of identity and provides social meaning. They confirm that dress can and is used to portray middle class identity.

On the contrary, Mabone did not feel the pressure to perform through dress. Mabone initially had the assumption that there was no Black middle class and that Black people who self-identified as middle class where snobbish. Thus, his lack of a need to impress them through dress was the performance of a proud working-class male identity. He reflected thus:

> *I experienced no other pressure to act accordingly within the data collection process. I dressed freely, and openly engaged the participants about my use of public transport.*

On one hand, Mabone's deliberate free dress was a form of resisting the idea that he had to fit in or that he was lacking. On the other hand, Leo recounted his negotiation of dress in encountering his participants thus:

> *I learnt to dress down when some of the participants came to the interviews in casual outfits. But this was a performance that rid me of my own dress consciousness because I love to dress nicely most times, irrespective of the occasion. I assumed I had to meet them at this level of casualness. Perhaps appearing casual is itself a middle class thing; I don't know.*

Thus, while Mabone did not experience any pressure with respect to dress performance, Leo, in his positioning within the Black middle class, was confronted with the casualness with which the participants attended interviews, a scenario he had to deal with and match. Thus, unlike Polite and Lesego who dressed up for acceptance, Leo found himself dressing down to adjust to members of this class in order not to appear "too serious". Surprisingly, Kris and Grace had no issues with the dress and creating an impression with the participants, this was because of their extensive experience as researchers and most importantly because of the firm middle class position as educated, professionals who are not badly paid.

Although there is an acknowledgement that, recently, men are starting to be expected to care about how they look (Kang et al., 2011; Leopeng and Langa 2019), it is less so for them than it is for women. Like many other social phenomena that stratify, women seem to have less choice when it comes to dressing in social interactions during the interviews. Ultimately, apart from Mabone; Lesego, Polite and Leo each had to perform middle classness in diverse ways by making dress decisions depending on their varied encounters with the participants, their backgrounds, and the perceptions they held of the Black middle class they were interviewing.

Do I Eat their Food? Performing Middle Class Generosity

When a person offers another something to eat or drink, this is considered an act of kindness, showing that the person making the offer is welcoming you into their space (Carling et al., 2014). In most Black families, guests are treated with such courtesy, even when the host family does not have anything fancy to offer. Thus, a cup of tea or glass of water serves this purpose, and this act is perceived as having good manners (Adam & Galinsky, 2012; Goffman, 1959). Below, Lesego reflected on this reality when she accepted such gestures from her participants:

> *When participants offered me food, I accepted the food because they were genuinely offering, and I saw*

it as a kind gesture. At home, I was always trained to offer something to visitors five minutes after their arrival. This is when I saw how I misjudged the Black middle class because I thought people with money are rude, not welcoming and unkind.

Bozalek (1999), in a seminal article on *Contextualising care in African families*, writes about reciprocal caring in extended families in the context of poverty and high apartheid. This type of caring illuminates the type of sharing Lesego mentions. This way of sharing was similarly experienced by Polite, who reflected thus:

Growing up in a township family in one context as a nuclear family and also having the privilege of growing up in an extended family context, my grandparents taught the family the importance of sharing; this applied mostly when it came to food. But it translated to other parts of my life, food is not just for you but others.

Having participants offer Lesego and Polite food meant they had good manners. Polite and Lesego come from a background where they were taught that when there is a visitor at home, they should be offered something to eat or drink, that food should be shared. For Lesego, her earlier negative perceptions of her participants changed at the point when they offered her food, as they were doing something, she was familiar with. The research process is very complex and when the researcher begins, they have preconceived notions about how the interviews will be encountered and perceptions about the participants. Nevertheless, when they actually conduct the interviews, some researchers' perceptions do change (Lisiak, 2015). This also shows that there is a cultural aspect that exists in performance.

Polite, however, dealt with this cultural obligation differently when she was at the receiving end of such food offers from members of the Black middle class she interviewed. In her words she reflected that:

> *Although the participants offered pleasantries such as coffee and food, the sense of pride of being a Sowetan girl came much into presence. I would insist on paying my own bill ... refusing food or drinks, even when I was hungry or thirsty, was my own way to show or display that their middle classness will not define parts of me in this process.*

There is clearly a conflict in Polite: although she understood the significance of sharing as it was taught to her in her family, she found it hard to accept the same sharing when it was offered by those who she considered better off than she was. Her refusal was a way of resisting how she assumed those who are better off will perceive young Black women from the township negatively.

Mabone, like Polite, was very resistant to the idea of a Black middle class at the beginning of the study. Although at the end Mabone conceded that there was a Black middle class, his earlier assumptions led him to reject offers of food and other pleasantries from the participants; he explained his experiences thus:

> *The Black middle class had a bewildering resistance to rejection. My defiance and rejection of their offers for food or drinks was opposed and questioned. I had to refuse; unexpectedly it eased the data collection process as it allowed interaction before the interviews commenced and gave me a chance to reinforce myself as a person. I still do not know why my thoughts about the*

> *Black middle class required me to be independent and able to pay for myself. It was fundamentally important that I remain their equals throughout the interaction. I had not experienced it in other academic or intellectual spaces, I often agreed to eat. However, my dislike of losing my independence was heightened within Black middle class data collection process.*

One notices, then, how both Polite and Mabone used refusal, particularly by insisting on paying for themselves, not only as a form of resistance but also to perform some sense of self-sufficiency. Rejecting the food and drinks offered was a form of self-preservation and working-class identity affirmation. This was a way to maintain agency and a tool to avert loss of power in the interview process. From Mabone's extract, for instance, we see that accepting the food would have positioned him as lower than the participants on the class strata. Mabone's initial ideas about the study participants were that, because of their class position, they were not Black enough; so, to maintain that stance he had to maintain his independence. He was keen to maintain his power and freedom and thus not be seen as dependent on the participants. Remaining independent, thus, was important for retaining equality with the participants, as well as not losing their identities.

In addition, when interviews are conducted in a public space like a restaurant, because it is a space where service is provided, it is, therefore, crucial for people to be buying customers. In most cases, participants would pay for the bill because they could afford it and did not mind. Research textbooks always state that participants should be offered something to drink if the interview is conducted at a public place like a restaurant or café (Babbie, 2004; Bless, Higson-Smith, & Sithole, 2014). When Lesego paid for the beverages it was appropriate as the interviewee was invited to participate in the research project and it was not as if Lesego was buying the participant but following research protocol.

However, for Mabone this being able to pay went beyond research protocol as suggested in research textbooks – it was about affirming that his working-class background was not a deficit. Mabone further played out this refusal and the notion of independence even in terms of his relationship with one of the research leaders. He reflected that:

> *I nonetheless resisted Prof Kris Marsh's assistance with Uber for distant or inconvenient interviews. I was not comfortable with the research leader's direct financial assistance. Both with Prof. Kris Marsh's Uber and participants' food offer, I struggled with the thought of obligation and dependency and declined offers I knew were well meant. It gave me freedom and confidence to articulate myself freely and equally at all times.*

Each team member was provided with research funds for travel to the interviews. However, the research leaders were aware that this money might not be enough as some of the interview locations were far and required multiple changes of transport and thus would be time consuming, hence the offer to pay for an Uber. However, even though Mabone argues that he was thus free and acted openly, his adamant refusal to be assisted or just offered the courtesy of a meal or drink was a way of performing to fit in with middle classness and illustrate equality with the participants. One could think of this as masculine performance even as Mabone, and other team members grappled with their identities in relation to members of the Black middle class.

Kris experienced no conflict with accepting food offered by the participants. It might have been a combination of her

American status, assumed middle class status, insider/outsider status or a combination of her statuses that informed how she approached offers for food. Kris reflected that:

> *For me, food was not an issue at all. I did not give it a second thought. If people offered me food, I took it. If the food was good, I would ask for seconds. If the food was not good, I forced myself to eat it simply to appear polite and considerate of the culture. Especially when it was food native to South Africa, such as tinned fish. That is one of my favorites that I experienced. As we all know the food that was great but did not agree with me was the "skop" [sheep's heads]. Anyways, and if the food was really really good, I would ask to take a plate with me.*

When we examine Kris's comments, she is suggesting that accepting food had no bearing on how she understood her middle classness. However, it seems that food did have some bearing. As an American, she wanted to be polite and respectful because that is the assumed behaviour of the middle class. For Kris, accepting food, consuming undesirable food and even taking food home are her direct social cues to demonstrate and perform her middle classness to those she interviewed. What informs Kris's perspective on performing middle classness derives from some of her previous knowledge on American Black middle class scholarship. For example, American sociologist Karyn Lacy, in her book *Blue-chip Black: race, class, and status in the new Black middle class* (2007) discusses notions of how Blacks develop an identity within their middle class group. The identity that influences the process of how the Black middle class individual will relate to the world around them. According to Lacy,

> *the key distinction between the white and black middle class is thus a matter of degree. Middle class Whites fit the public image of the middle class and may therefore take their middle class status for granted, but Blacks who have 'made it' must work harder, more deliberately, and more consistently to make their middle class status known to others.* (2007, p. 3).

Lacy points out that the Black middle class must also take upon themselves a new identity to properly conceptualise themselves as Black middle class. They must endure the conflict of "making it" and "being Black" (Lacy, 2007, p. 8).

On the other hand, Grace did not receive offers of food. This might have been because she interviewed most participants at their workplaces or at Kris's place in Melrose Arch. She was, however, offered water and, at times, tea. What struck her was the generosity the participants showed in terms of sharing their time. She shared the following reflection to illustrate:

> *I was surprised that the participants with the positions they occupy were willing to make time to be interviewed. I always assumed that wealthy Blacks are not interested in sharing their experiences. This assumption is influenced by the fact that most research in South Africa is done on the poor and the reason provided is that people from Sandton with their high walls are seldom available, so I was both surprised and thankful for their generosity.*

Interviewing up is usually a challenge because of time factors and access issues. However, in our case, it was proved that the middle class and the higher middle class are amenable to contributing to knowledge production.

MIDDLE CLASS PERFORMANCE TO GAIN ACCESS TO THE BLACK MIDDLE CLASS

Besides reflecting on our performance during the interviews, as a research team, we had to acknowledge that prior middle class performance was consciously or subconsciously used to gain access to middle class spaces, events and networks. Grace and Kris provide vivid accounts of this access during one of the final research team meetings. They reflected in the following way;

Grace noted:

Wow! So, we've done 88 interviews. Um, started the interviews beginning of August and we had six people working on the project. So, can we just share some of the experiences? I mean, I, I know that the experience was, interesting and quite informative for me. I learned a lot, um, and not only about, you know, doing research on the black middle class, but for personal development. Because I think we interviewed a lot of interesting people that had, a lot to share, you know, in terms of how they, they are making it. Um, and what the challenges they have experienced are. And at the personal level, I felt that I took a lot from that ... Uh, but also in terms of the Black middle class, I also felt that .... if I was doing the recruitment for the project, I would not have recruited the people that Kris recruited. And I think that is an important thing to think about. How, how you are positioned influences how you do research. How you, how you interact with people, which people you will interact with, and therefore it will shape the kind of study you have at the end. So, I thought that was a, a significant thing

> *for me. ... thinking about the people that I would have, you know, recruited; the places that I visit and all that. I would have had a very different, sample, and I thought that is worth thinking about and noting as we reflect, on the project.*

The insider–outsider dynamic played an important role in thinking about this question. Although Kris's American status made her an outsider, it was positive for her ability to recruit without bias as she did not know or have any preconceived ideas about most of the individuals she contacted for the purpose of the study. Her insiderness, which can be articulated as her middle classness and her American citizenship allowed her access to live in an upper middle class area during her Fulbright fellowship in South Africa. These two dynamics influenced the types of participants she was able to recruit for the study. Kris shared similar sentiments to Grace, and was constantly questioning how her American status and automatically-assumed middle class status shaped the recruitment process. In her reflections Kris agrees with Grace and notes that:

> *kind of to dovetail what you're [Grace] saying because I am American, I think I have American privilege and that allowed me into spaces that I wouldn't normally have access to and so we got access to people that I didn't think we would necessarily get access to. And I think also being American and living where I live, I run, I run into people on that upper end of the Black middle class, as well. So that kind of made our demographic much more diverse, because of where I am staying and because I am an American. And I think also, thirdly, I think because I am an American and I just don't know people, there's people that, the*

> *girls were telling me like, "Do you know who this is?" I'm like, "No. That's just somebody that I ran into." So, I was kind of fearless because I was fearless, but I was also kind of naïve. I just didn't know these people. Had I known them, I probably would've been a little timid and not really want to talk to them. But there were people that I saw at the gym or people I saw walking, having coffee and so, I didn't have any fear because I just didn't know them. But had I known, I'd probably be much more intimidated or much more, um, reserved at talking to them.*

As a whole, the research team acknowledged the insider–outsider dynamic throughout the entire research process and even continued to reflect on this dynamic in post-interview research team meeting discussions. Grace further explained that:

> *You know. That, that, you know, the outsider-insider dynamic. It's real, and, and sometimes we think about it in ways that don't emphasize that when you're an outsider, you have a lot of advantage, in, especially those ways as well.*

While the advantage of getting 88 interviews was the outsider–insider dynamic and the middle class performance by Kris, the American on the team, the research team also discussed the drawbacks. For example, Kris discussed her outsider status by suggesting the following:

> *… when I first got here, I was meeting people; I was having coffee with them; I was telling them about the study, asking them to sign up. I kind of wish I didn't do that as much. I appreciate it because it yielded us 88 interviews, but I kind of felt like*

> *I couldn't really get a chance to interview a lot of people because I had a relationship with them?
> ... And so, I'm not as immersed in the data as you guys are because you did more interviews than I did.*

While the research team saw this as a possible drawback, Lesego brought up an issue echoed by the research team. It was the idea that the respondents assumed that since Kris recruited them, "*...they also thought they were going to be interviewed by Prof Kris*". So Lesego shared that it was intimidating when some of the participants were shocked that Kris was not the one to interview them. Their shock affected the beginning of the interview negatively. Lesego had the following reflection to share:

> *I'm the same way as, um, you know I'm gonna be "Who are you? What are you doing? How do you come in to the study? Are you that important? Are you important like Kris? Do you come from America?" You know, those questions you asked. And I thought there was a point in time I, because at some point I was intimidated, I felt intimidated, because these are big people. I even told you that for me, this is like solid, solid middle class! This is not just your general middle class that you meet every day, because these are big people, people that own Pick n Pay.*

In the above quote by Lesego it is also interesting to note how she refers to the different strata in the middle class when she says,

> *these are big people. I even told you that for me, this is like solid, solid middle class! This is not just your general middle class that you meet every day.*

She uses the word solid to refer to the strata of individuals we interviewed, thus suggesting that they might not be as precarious as what she calls, "*your general middle class that you meet every day*". This distinction is also indicative of who Lesego is in the class hierarchy where she lives and the types of people she meets every day. One of the factors that contributed to Kris being able to recruit the kinds of people she did was because for her they were the types of people she met every day at Melrose Arch. Therefore, social context generally and the social location of the researcher matters for recruitment of study participants and how we will theorise as well.

Grace also experienced the shock that Lesego talks about in the earlier quote. One of the participants who were clearly not happy to be interviewed by anyone other than Kris made her wait for an hour. After the hour Grace had to leave as she had another meeting in Tshwane. Even though that could have influenced her experience of the interviews negative she reflected on this experience thus:

> *Yes. But I also thought about how … and I think you, you also picked up on that. I think all of us have picked up on how generous they were. I didn't expect it of them.*

Grace was also surprised that their generosity went beyond them giving their time but included their well wishes. She reflected that:

> *For me, I didn't expect that they would be so giving, you know. I mean, you spoke to them for two hours, many of them were so generous, not only with their time and their stories, but they also wanted us to do well. They wanted the project to do well.*

This idea that they were generous beyond our initial assumptions was also shared by Mabone, who said the following at the final meeting:

> *They were generous. I didn't expect it when you interview up. Honesty. I expected they are going to hide things because I'm interviewing now.*

The general perceptions that those who are wealthy are snobbish influenced our preconceived ideas and thus our surprise that they were willing to open up and share not only their time but also their experiences. Mabone had this to further say on his experience:

> *I expected the judgment. Instead, they, after the interviews, they felt like they could talk and share. I expected I should be the one to be humble. All these people ... are financially literate. That's why, that's the way they are now*

Mabone in the above quote clearly illustrates that his earlier preconceived ideas that the Black middle class are snobbish and unapproachable had shifted. Lesego's reflections also illustrate a similar shift. Again, the previous discussions in this chapter suggest that both us as a research team and the respondents for the study were, at times, engaging in some type of middle class performance, from the respondents agreeing to be interviewed to the research team deciding what clothing to wear to what food they should consume.

While Kris did the recruiting, she was concerned about some cultural differences, as an American might come off as not knowledgeable about the culture and ultimately not be viewed as middle class by the participants. She expressed her concerns around the notion of language. She reflected that;

> *Well, for me, um, people would say stuff [phrases, concepts and ideas] in, in a different language ... And be like "Okay. What I mean by this..." so they would just say it. They would just say it. They would just jump out and say it. I'm like, sitting there like "Okay." (laughing) But this means blah, blah, blah, blah, blah.*

Kris explained the respondents would see her confusion or how uncomfortable she had become with a phrase, concept or idea that was expressed in indigenous languages, so the respondent would say something like "*it comes out better this way ... and then I'll translate it*". In other words, some terms are best captured in the native language of the speaker and then they will translate. While Kris was thankful for the respondent educating her on the phrase, concept or idea, she wondered if the respondents were second-guessing her preparedness for the interview and the research project and ultimately challenging her middle class status and performance.

Kris was thus often confronted with whether words in the native tongues were discounting her culturally and through language or making her second guess her own notions of being prepared as a scholar attempting to study the South African Black middle class. Kris notes how she was not sure if statements made by respondents should be probed further or was it a lack of preparation on her part? She reflected in the following way:

> *So, I was like "Oh, okay." But for me also, it wasn't a language thing, it was a cultural thing. I was like "Okay. Is this a probe or is this something I should know? I don't want to be here and not just have a general knowledge*

about the culture, because somebody said something about their Zulu culture. I was like "Okay, am I supposed to just know what that is?" Should I probe it, should I not ask 'because I don't know, because I was really thinking - like, say that - I'm like, you don't know what a clever black means (laughing) so I didn't want to come out with "Well what do you mean by that?" And they're like "What? You don't know?" (laughing). Sometimes people say stuff and I was like "Okay, please explain" and I was glad I did say something, because I was gonna let it go and I was like "well, I guess I figure out what this 'clever Black' is." Yeah, because I was still, something was like, I think I should probably know this. I'm not gonna probe. What do you mean by this? I have to Google it later. (laughing)

MELROSE ARCH

One concern that we had as a research team was the location of some of the interviews at Kris's apartment in Melrose Arch. By way of context, Melrose Arch is a mixed-use space with private residences, upscale retail, fine dining and a five-star hotel located in the wealthier northern suburbs of Johannesburg. The northern suburbs of Johannesburg are the historically wealthiest locations in the city and remains so in contemporary South Africa. Kris expressed the group's concern by posing a question:

How do we feel about doing the interviews at Melrose Arch? Do you think that in some ways that the space influence the responses?" To this Leo

> *responded that "It made my last participant very nervous.*

Leo, then went on to express how the respondent performed middle classness differently when inside Kris's apartment and outside of the same apartment. Leo said an English accent was "performed" in the apartment and during the interview which was dropped once the interview was over. Leo reflected further that:

> *There was a language - so, the young lady is - she grew up in [Soweto], um, and when you speak to her outside, outside the interview, it doesn't bring in accent, but when she was in the apartment there was an accent. So… (laughing)*

Leo finished his statement with laughter. It seems clear that both the researcher and the subject were concerned with what it means to be Black middle class and thus how to perform influenced the accent during the interview. For this respondent, it meant a certain type of language that demonstrates I am middle class and the respondent felt an English accent gave her the social capital needed to secure herself a position in the Black middle class. Ndletyana (2014) notes that as part of the project of "civilizing" Blacks during colonialism and apartheid, educated Blacks had to play the part illustrated through how they dressed and articulated the Queen's English. This performance of an English accent, as experienced by Leo, is clearly a remnant of that history. Such social performance confers privilege and access.

While some respondents changed their behaviour while in the apartment, others who were in awe of the place even decided to look around. Lesego said:

> *I had participants who would, like, go through [the apartment] and just look at me and like "Wow.*

This is the nicest apartment ever". And there was, this one was very comfortable, it was like "Hm. You too, you too much lady." She went out and like looked at the [entire apartment], and you can't say no, don't do it (laughing).

Polite agreed with Lesego, noting that:

I had one that was upstairs and consider the upstairs gym as their own. They considered it like a personal gym. I was like ... Oh, it's not your place.

The team had to explain to the respondents, especially those that were being "too comfortable" that the apartment belonged to Kris. For Kris, she felt that those respondents that were comfortable with the apartment where either solid middle class, familiar with such spaces or entry-level Black middle class and learning to manoeuvre middle class spaces. This manoeuvring and performing middle class Blackness include giving the impression that they are comfortable and familiar will middle class status. Whether the apartment in Melrose Arch made the respondents comfortable or not is an interesting discussion, but it is more interesting to consider that the place might have biased the respondents' responses. The apartment was definitely in an upper middle class area. The unanswered question is, therefore, whether the location of the apartment, as well as the apartment itself, caused people to give socially desirable answers. Furthermore, did they feel the pressure to perform a certain type of middle classness because of the location of the interview?

CONCLUSION

The intention of this chapter was to provide reflexive discussions on how the research team performed middle classness in order to fit in with or to affirm their individual positioning. The discussion illustrates that because how we look matters socially it influenced how we dressed or not dressed for the interview. The research team clearly understood the costs of not looking appropriate. Thus, the politics of acceptability and respectability were either consciously or unconsciously played out. This was further done in encounters with and response to being offered food and other forms of niceties. The research encounter is a microcosm of interactions in the broader society. This is illustrated in how dress is used as a marker of equality and acceptance at one point and how in another it is used to affirm differences. Another important marker of equality performed by the team was the use of education to mask our deficit of class position. This was done so as to feel good and thus able to perform the task of knowledgeable and acceptable interviewer.

In conclusion, this chapter has illustrated how performance of middle classness through dress and announcement of education levels was used to gain access. This performance we conclude was also used to affirm self in congruence with our preconceived ideas of the research phenomenon and the study participants.

6

CONCLUSION

The discussion in the chapters above made two contributions to knowledge. First, it explores how Black South Africans living in South Africa conceptualise middle classness. Second, it demonstrates how this conceptualisation informs our own social identity, as researchers and our own standings within the Black middle class.

Social scientists remain concerned with how the history of legalised racial segregation and discrimination, such as the system of apartheid in South Africa, currently affects Blacks as individuals. This book focused on enriching theoretical perspectives on race and class from the perspective of the interviewee/interviewer interaction as well as the outsider/insider dynamic. It contextualised both subjective and objective definitions of middle class while highlighting the constantly and vastly shifting conceptualisation and operationalisation of this term.

The book provides a complex portrait of the evolving Black middle class in the twenty-first century via an unusual lens. As researchers, we engaged with our experiences of fieldwork in interviewing the Black middle class in South Africa. It has highlighted the complexities among the research team in conceptualising the term Black middle class. Unlike other works, this book delves into the iterative processes of theorising what it means to be middle class with Black researchers studying the Black middle class. Researchers seldom present this perspective. We centred our reflections on the journey as researchers interacting with the Black middle class in South Africa. These reflections give a unique approach to understanding the researchers' subjectivity in the knowledge production process which reflects the lived experiences of the South African middle class. The book draws on historical, national and international social science literature for theoretical grounding. Previous theories and conceptualisations of the Black middle class shapes this book's analytical approach and understanding of how researchers engage (or not) with the Black middle class while understanding how their perceptions shape data collection and analysis.

For more specific conclusions we turn to each chapter. In Chapter 2: *The Black middle class: a conceptual moving target*, two central conclusions emerge. First, looking closely at the larger social science literature, we conclude that the Black middle class has and continues to experience marginalisation, discrimination and segregation. Second, similar to the observations of Krige (2012) and Alexander, Ceruti, Motseke, Phadi, and Wale (2013), we assert that the Black middle class is making steady but very slow progress on social mobility as poor Blacks continue to slide further down that same ladder.

As a research team, we constantly took a critical view of our own socio-economic identities. By interrogating our own difficulties with conceptualising the Black middle class and self-identification with the Black middle class position, this book contributes to the on-going debates about conceptualising this class in more nuanced ways. This discussion of our own personal engagement with the term as we were partaking in the interview processes provides an opportunity to think differently about theory building in Black middle class scholarship.

In Chapter 3: *Those snobbish "clever" Blacks: Preconceived notions of the Black middle class*, we conclude that the insider and outsider dynamics of the researcher play an important part in affecting interviews with the Black middle class and the knowledge production in Black middle class scholarship. Our preconceived ideas were challenged in some ways and affirmed in other ways. When we interacted with the participants, we were less likely to hold stereotypical views about members of the Black middle class. Fusch and Ness (2015) see this shift as important as it allows the researcher to "hear and interpret the behavior of others". Without including this reflexivity exercise in the research process, as a research team we run the risk of allowing our preconceived ideas to cloud our judgement and become the force that drives the social research. On another note, the theoretical stance provided by Collins (1986) in *Learning from the outsider within: The sociological significance of Black feminist thought*, we recognise that the various positions we held with regards to insider–outsider positions were useful in our reflexive endeavours. These diverse positions concerning the Black middle class position and our identification with different genders were useful in allowing us to engage in critical and creative reflexivity.

In Chapter 4: *Thank you, but I got this: Gender dynamics between researchers and the Black middle class*, we conclude that in social research there exist gender dynamics between the researcher and the researched, in which these dynamics have had an influence on the Black middle class project. Looking at gender for this book is of significant value because, in South Africa, the Black middle class belong to other social categories such as age, gender, citizenship, education, ethnicity, income, sexual orientation, socioeconomic status and immigration and these social identities in the research field provide privilege for some and marginalise others in the process. It is, therefore, important to reflect on how gender dynamics have been reflected by the research team.

In Chapter 5: *What do I wear and do I eat their food? Performing middle classness*, we assert that performance of those who are involved in the study has an impact on the research process, particularly the physical appearance – the dress code – of the participants and the researcher and how individuals act out during the interview process. For instance, accepting or rejecting food, a ride or other "favors" is highly influenced by our own individual assumptions, beliefs, perceptions and feelings during the research process and played a role in our reflections as the research team.

We suggest future research on the Black middle class. We admonish scholars to consider how their presence informs the research process. Given the issues faced by middle class Blacks in particular, which we stated throughout the book, researchers should compare and analyse the historical context and the current socio-economic similarities and differences of the Black middle class in a global framework.

The Black middle class has been extensively studied, picked apart and scrutinised, from the early work *Black bourgeoisie* by Frazier (1957) to more current analyses such as *Class in Soweto* by Alexander et al. (2013) and *The new Black middle class* by Southall (2016). These scholars have put this demographic group under the microscope to better understand their values, class identity and their behaviour. These books and similar Black middle class scholarship explore issues of racial and economic inequality in one form or another, but cast only a tangential light on researchers studying the Black middle class. Omitting the voice of the researcher has two potential drawbacks. First, excluding the researcher prevents

Conclusion

a broader and more encompassing view of the Black middle class. Second, overlooking the view of the researcher ignores the understanding of how researchers influence the knowledge production process of defining the Black middle class. This book builds from these seminal works and makes unique contributions by exploring the Black middle class from the researchers' perspective.

BIBLIOGRAPHY

Adam, H., & Galinsky, A. D. (2012). Enclothed cognition. *Journal of Experimental Social Psychology, 48*(4), 918–925.

Adichie, C. N. (2017). *Dear ijeawele: Or a feminist manifesto fifteen suggestions*. London: Harper Collins Publishers.

Alexander, P., Ceruti, C., Motseke, K., Phadi, M., & Wale, K. (2013). *Class in Soweto*. South Africa: University of KwaZulu-Natal Press.

Allport, G. W., Clark, K., & Pettigrew, T. (1954). *The nature of prejudice*. Garden City, NY: Doubleday.

Ampofo, A. A., Beoku-Betts, J., & Osirim M. J. (2008). Researching African women and gender studies: New social science perspectives. *African and Asian Studies 7*, 327–341.

Babbie, E. R. (2004). *The basics of social research* (10th ed.). Belmont, CA: Wadsworth Publishing.

Babu, T. D. (2015). *Marketing to the emerging black middle class in South Africa: An in-depth exploration of the lives of young black professional women*. MBA dissertation, Stellenbosch University.

Beall, J., Crankshaw, O., & Parnell, S. (2002). *Uniting a divided city: Governance and social exclusion in Johannesburg*. London: Earthscan Publications Ltd.

Bendix, R., & Lipset, S. M. (1953). *Class, status, and power: A reader in social stratification*. Glencoe, IL: The Free Press.

Berger, R. (2015). Now I see it, now I don't: Researcher's position and reflexivity in qualitative research. *Qualitative Research*, *15*(2), 219–234.

Berry, B. (2016). *The power of looks: Social stratification of physical appearance*. Chicago, IL: Routledge.

Besteman, C. (2008). *Transforming Cape Town*. Berkley, CA: University of California Press.

Bettie, J. (2014). *Women without class: Girls, race and identity*. Oakland, CA: University of California Press.

Bless C, Higson-Smith, C., & Sithole, S. L. (2014). Fundamentals of social research methods: An African perspective. Cape Town, South Africa: Juta and Company Ltd.

Blumer, H. (1969). Fashion: From class differentiation to collective selection. *The Sociological Quarterly*, *10*, 275–291.

Bourdieu, P. (1986). *Distinction*. London: Routledge.

Bourdieu, P. (1996). *Distinction: A social critique of the judgement of taste*. Cambridge: Harvard University Press.

Bowser, B. (2007). *The black middle class: Social mobility and vulnerability*. Boulder, CO: Lynne Rienner Publishers.

Bozalek, V. (1999). Contextualizing caring in black South African families. *Social Politics: International Studies in Gender, State & Society*, *6*(1), 85–99.

Bundy, C. (1988). *The rise and the fall of the South African peasantry* (2nd ed.). Cape Town, South Africa: David Phillip.

Burger R., Steenekamp C., Van der Berg S., & Zoch A. (2014). The middle class in post-apartheid South Africa: Examining and comparing rival approaches. Stellenbosch, South Africa: Department of Economics, Stellenbosch University.

Burger, R., McAravey, C., & Van der Berg. S. (2015). *The capability threshold: Re-examining the definitions of the middle class in an unequal developing country.* Stellenbosch Economic Working Papers: 16/15. Department of Economics, Stellenbosch University, Stellenbosch, South Africa.

Butler, J. (2009). Performativity, precarity, and sexual politics. *Revista de Antropología Iberoamericana*, 4(3), i–xiii.

Canham, H., & Williams, R. (2017). Being black, middle class and the object of two gazes. *Ethnicities*, 17(1), 23–46. Retrieved form https://doi.org/10.1177/1468796816664752

Carling, J., Bivand Erdal, M., & Ezzati, R. (2014). Beyond the insider-outsider divide in migration. *Migration Studies*, 2(1), 36–54.

Carter, P. L. (2005). *Keepin' it real: School success beyond Black and White.* New York, NY: Oxford University Press.

Chigumadzi, P. (2019). Why I am no longer to Nigerians about race. Retrieved from https://www.africasacountry.com/2019/04/why-im-no-longer-talking-to-nigerians-about-race

Collins, P. H. (1986). Learning from the outsider within: The sociological significance of Black feminist thought. *Social Problems*, 33(6), 14–32.

Collins, P. H. (1997). Comment on Hekman's "Truth and method: Feminist standpoint theory revisited': Where's the power? *Signs: Journal of Women in Culture and Society*, 22(2), 375–381.

Collins, S. (1997). Black corporate executives: The making and breaking of a black middle class. Philadelphia, PA: Temple Press.

Collins, P. H. (2000). *Black feminist thought: Knowledge, consciousness and the politics of empowerment* (2nd ed.). New York, NY: Routledge.

Crenshaw, K. (1991). Mapping the margins: Intersectionality, identity politics, and violence against women of color. *Stanford Law Review*, 43, 1241–1299.

Crankshaw, O. (1997). Race, class and the changing division of labour under apartheid. *Contemporary Sociology*, 27, 47–48.

Crankshaw, O. (2008). Race, space and the post-fordist spatial order of Johannesburg. *Urban Studies*, 45(8), 1692–1711.

Darity, W. A., Jr. & Mason, P. L. (2004). Evidence on discrimination in employment: Codes of color, codes of gender. *African American urban experience: Perspectives from the colonial period to the present* (pp. 156–186). New York, NY: Palgrave Macmillan US.

de Coninck, L. (2018). The uneasy boundary work of 'coconuts' and 'black diamonds': Middle- class labelling in post-apartheid South Africa. *Critical African Studies*, 10, 155–172. doi:10.1080/21681392.2018.1516366

de Vullers, J. (2019). "Joburg no longer pays top salaries - or has the most jobs" Business Insider, February, 06, 2019.

Dow, D. M. (2019). *Mothering while black: Boundaries and burdens of middle-class parenthood*. Berkeley, CA: University of California Press.

Du Bois, W. E. B. (1899). *The Philadelphia Negro: A social study*. Philadelphia, PA: University of Pennsylvania.

Fanon, F. (1952). *Black skin white masks*. England: Pluto Press.

Feagin, J., & Sikes, M. (1997). *Living with racism: The black middle-class*. Boston, MA: Beacon Press.

Finlay, L. (2002). "Outing" the researcher: The provenance, process, and practice of reflexivity. *Qualitative Health Research, 12*(4), 531–545.

Fox, N. (2009). *Using interviews in a research project*. East Midlands, England: NIHR.

Frazier, F. (1957). *Black bourgeoisie*. New York, NY: Simon and Schuster.

Fulton D., Furman, D., & Finlay, N. (2014). A longitudinal study of the middle class: Growth, size and marketing strategies. *Research in Business and Economics Journal, 10*(1), 1–20.

Fusch, P. I., & Ness, L. R. (2015). Are we there yet? Data saturation in qualitative research. *The Qualitative Report, 20*(9), 1408–1416. Retrieved from http://nsuworks.nova.edu/tqr/vol20/iss9/3

Gill, H., Purru, K., & Lin, G. (2012). In the midst of participatory action research practices: Moving towards decolonizing and decolonial praxis. *Reconceptualizing Educational Research Methodology, 3*(1). Retrieved form https://doi.org/10.7577/rerm.357

Goffman, E. (1959). *The presentation of self in everyday life*. Garden City, NY: Doubleday.

Gopalda, A. (2013). Intersectionality 101. *Journal of Public Policy & Marketing, 32*, 90–94.

Gqola, P. (2017). *Reflecting rogue: Inside the mind of a feminist*. Johannesburg, South Africa: MF Books Joburg.

Gronnerod, J. S. 2004. On the meanings and uses of laughter in research interviews. *Young, 12*(1), 31–49.

Hare, N. (1965). In O. C. Cox (Ed.), *Introduction*. New York, NY: Marzani & Munsell.

Harries, B. (2016). What's sex got to do with it? When a woman asks questions. *Women's Studies International Forum, 59*, 48–57.

Hesse-Biber, S., & Leavy, P. (2011). *The practice of qualitative research* (2nd ed.). London: Sage.

Higginbotham, E. B. (1993). *Righteous discontent: The women's movement in the black baptist church, 1880–1920*. Cambridge, MA: Harvard University Press.

hooks, B. (2000). *Feminist theory: From margin to center* (2nd ed.). Cambridge, MA: South End Press.

Hoosen, F., & Mafukidze. (2007). *Land use management and democratic governance in the city of Johannesburg*. Pretoria, South Africa: Human Science Research Council: Rural and Economic Development Department.

Hung, A. A., Andrew, M., Parker, J., & Yoong, K. (2009). *Defining and measuring*. RAND Working Paper Series WR-708. RAND Corporation, CA.

Hunt, M. O., & Ray, R. (2012). Social class identification among black Americans: Trends and determinants, 1974–2010. *American Behavioral Scientist*, 0002764212458275.

Ibanga, E. (2007). Utilization of French graduates in secondary school in Makurdi local government area of Benue state of Nigeria. *Journal of Technology and Education in Nigeria, 12*(2), 40–44.

James, D. (2014). "Deeper into a hole?" Borrowing and lending in South Africa. *Current Anthropology, 55*(S9), S17–S29.

Järviluoma, H., Moisala, P., & Vilkko, A. (2011). *Gender and the fieldwork*. London: Sage Publications.

Jewkes, R., Dunkle, K., Nduna, M., Levin, J., Jama, N., Khuzwayo, N., … Duvvury, N. (2016). Factors associated with HIV zero-status in young rural South African women: Connections between intimate partner violence and HIV. *International Journal of Epidemiology, 35*(6), 1461–1468. Retrieved from https://doi.org/10.1093/ije/dyl218

Johnson, K., Lennon, S. J., & Rudd, N. (2014). Dress, body and self: Research in the social psychology of dress. *Fashion and Textiles, 1*(1), 20.

Jones, J. (2010). *Labor of love, labor of sorrow: Black women, work and the family, from slavery to the present*. New York, NY: Basic Books.

Kang, M., Sklar, M., & Johnson, K. P. (2011). Men at work: Using dress to communicate identities. *Journal of Fashion Marketing and Management, 15*(4), 412–427.

Khunou, G. (2015a). What middle class? The shifting and dynamic nature of class position. *Development Southern Africa, 31*(1), 90–103.

Khunou, G. (2015b). 'Shaky ground: The challenge of being black and middle class'. The Conversation, 11 May.

Khunou, G. (2015c). *South Africa's emergent middle class*. New York, NY: Routledge.

Khunou, G., Phaswana, E., Khoza-Shangase, K., & Canham, H. (2019). Black academic voices: The South African experience. Pretoria, South Africa: HSRC Press.

Khunou, G. (n.d). Interviewing women and men in the South African maintenance system: Some experiences.

King E., & Horrocks, C. (2010). *Interviews in qualitative research*. London: Sage.

Kitis, E, Milani, D., & Levon, E. (2018). 'Black diamonds', 'clever blacks' and other metaphors: Constructing the South African print media. *Discourse & Communication*, 12(2), 149–170. doi:10.1177/1750481317745750

Krige, D. (2011). *Power, identity and agency at work in the popular economies of Soweto and Black Johannesburg*. PhD dissertation, University of Witwatersrand. Retrieved form http://wiredspace.wits.ac.za/handle/10539/10143

Krige, D. (2012). The changing dynamics of social class, mobility and housing in black Johannesburg. *Alternation*, 19(1), 19–45.

Krige, D. (2015). 'Growing up' and 'moving up': Metaphors that legitimise upward mobility. *Development Southern Africa*, 32(1), 104–117.

Kros, C. (2010). *The seed of separate development*. Pretoria, South Africa: UNISA Press.

Lacy, K. R. (2007). *Blue-chip black: Race, class, and status in the new black middle class*. Berkeley, CA: University of California Press.

Landry, B. (1987). *The new black middle class*. Berkeley, CA: University of California Press.

Landry, B. (2018). The new black middle class in the twenty-first century. New Brunswick, Canada: Rutgers University Press.

Lemanski, C. (2006). The impact of residential desegregation on social integration: Evidence from a South African neighborhood. *Geoforum*, *37*(3), 417–435. doi:10.1016/j. geoforum.2005.09.002

Leopeng, B., & Langa, M. (2018). Black middle class masculinities in postapartheid South Africa: Consumerism, fashion and the portrayal of masculine identities in destiny magazine. *Fashion Theory*, *23*(1), 57–83.

Leopeng, B., & Langa, M. (2019). Black Middle-class Masculinities in Postapartheid South Africa: Consumerism, Fashion and the Portrayal of Masculine Identities in Destiny Man Magazine. *Fashion Theory, 23*(1), 57-83.

Lisiak, A. (2015). 'Fieldwork and fashion: Gendered and classed performances in research sites'. *Forum: Qualitative Social Research*, *16*(2).

Lucal, B. (1999). What it means to be gendered me: Life on the boundaries of a dichotomous gender system. *Gender and Society*, *13*, 781–797. doi:10.1177/089124399014006006

Lyons, L., & Chipperfield, J. (2000). (De) constructing the interview: A critique of the participatory model. *Resources for Feminist Research*, *28*, 33–48.

Mabandla, N. (2013). *Lahla Nguba: The continuities and discontinuities of South African black middle class*. South Africa: Afrika- Studiecentrum.

Mama, A. (2005). Gender studies for Africa's intellectual transformation. In T. Mkandawire (Ed.), *African intellectuals: Rethiinking politics, language, gender and development*. London: Zed Press.

Manderson, L., & Block, E. (2016). Relatedness and care in Southern Africa and beyond. *Social Dynamics*, *42*(2), 205–217. doi:10.1080/02533952.2016.1218139

Marsh, K., Darity, W., Cohen, P. N., Casper, L. M., & Salters, D. (2007). The emerging black middle class: Single and living along. *Social Forces, 86*(2), 735–762.

Martin, P. Y. (2003). "Said and done" versus "saying and doing": Gendering practices, practicing gender at work. *Gender & Society, 17,* 342. doi:10.117/0891243203017003002

Martin, J. H. (2005). Interviewer-administered primary data collection. In D. H. Tustin, A. A. Ligthelm, J. H. Martins, & H. J. Van Wyk (Eds.), *Marketing research in practice.* Pretoria, South Africa: University of South Africa.

Marx, K. (1984). *Capital: A critique of political economy* (Vol. II). London: Lawrence & Wishart.

Mattes, R. (2002). Democracy without the people. *Journal of Democracy, 13*(1), 22–36.

Mattes, R. (2014). *South African's emerging black middle class: A harbinger of political change?* WIDER Working Paper 2014/147. World Institute for Development Economics Research, Helsinki.

Maxwell, M. L., Abrams, J., Zungu, T., & Mosavel, M. (2016). Conducting community-engaged qualitative research in South Africa: Memoirs of intersectional identities abroad. *Qualitative Research, 16*(1), 95–110.

Melber, H. (2013). Africa and the middle class (es). *Africa Spectrum, 48*(3), 111–120.

Melber, H. (2017). *The rise of the Africa's middle class.* South Africa: Wits University Press.

Moore, D. D. (2015). Experiences of being an insider and an outsider during a qualitative study with men who have experienced significant weight loss. *The Qualitative Report, 20*(1), 87–106.

Moynihan, D. P., Rainwater, L., & Yancey, W. L. (1967). *The Negro family: The case for national action* (p. 23). Cambridge, MA: MIT Press.

Mtshelwane, D., Nel, J. A., & Brink, L. (2016). Impression management within the Zulu culture: Exploring tactics in the work context. *SA Journal of Industrial Psychology*, *42*(1), 1–13.

Murray, N. (1992). Colombus and the USA: From mythology to ideology. *Race & Class*, *33*(3), 49–65.

Naples, N. A. (1996). A feminist revisiting of the insider/outsider debate: The "outsider phenomenon" in rural Iowa. *Qualitative Sociology*, *19*(1), 83–106.

Ndelu, S. (2017). *In their voices: Being (Trans) gender diverse at a South African university*. South Africa: TUF.

Ndinga-Kangaanga, M. (2019). Towards an understanding of 'Black tax' and the Black middle class. Business Maverick, May 7, 2019.

Ndletyana, M. (2014). *Middle class in South Africa: Significance, role and impact*. Unpublished paper presented at the BRICS 6th Academic Forum, Brazil.

Nduna, M., Skweyiya, Y., Khunou, G., Pambo, V., & Mdletshe, T. (2015). Ethical reflections in qualitative research on father absence from South Africa. In *Social Science Research Ethics for a Globalizing World* (pp. 223–240). Abingdon: Routledge.

Ngoma, A. L. (2015). *Political identity repertoires of South Africa's professional black middle class*. MA dissertation, University of the Witwatersrand.

Nuttall S. (2004). Girl bodies. *Social Text*, *78*, 17–33.

Oakley, A. (2016). Interviewing women again: Power, time and the gift. *Sociology*, *50*(1), 195–213.

Oyewumi, O. (1997). *The invention of a women. Making an African sense of western gender discourses.* Minneapolis, MN: University of Minnesota Press.

Oyewumi (2002). Conceptualizing gender: The Eurocentric foundation of feminist concepts and the challenges of African epistemologies. *JENda: A Journal of Culture and Women Studies*, 2(1), 1–9.

Pattillo-McCoy, M. (1999). *Black picket fences.* Chicago, IL: University of Chicago Press.

Pattillo-McCoy, M. (2013). *Black picket fences: Privilege and peril among the black middle class.* Chicago, IL: University of Chicago Press.

Peires, J. B. (1989). *The dead will arise nongqawuse and the great Xhosa cattle killing movement of 1856.* Bloomington, IN: Indiana University Press.

Petrovski, S. (2018). *Gender perceptions through unisex names: A research paper.* Accessed 1 March 2019. Retrieved from https://medium.com/@stxfn/gender-perception-through-unisex-names-a-research-paper-704ea0aee4d4

Phadi, M. (2010). *Phakati: Soweto's middling class. Documentary made by Eyelight productions and the centre of sociological research.* Johannesburg, South Africa: University of Johannesburg.

Phadi, M., & Manda, O. (2010). The language of class: Southern Sotho and Zulu meanings of 'middle class' in Soweto. *South African Review of Sociology*, 41(3), 81.

Phadi, M., & Ceruti, C. (2011). Multiple meanings of the middle class in Soweto, South Africa. *African Sociological Review / Revue Africaine de Sociologie*, 15(1), 87–107.

Posel, D. (2010). Races to consume: Revisiting South Africa's history of race, consumption and the struggle for freedom. *Ethnic and Racial Studies*, *33*(2), 157–175.

Rapoport, R., & Rapoport, R. N. (1976). *Dual-career families re-examined: New integrations of work and family*. London: Martin Robertson.

Regulska, J. (2018). The #MeToo movement as a global learning moment. *International Higher Education*, *94*, 5–6. doi:10.6017/ihe.2018.0.10554

Reid, A., Brown, J. M., Smith, J. M., Cope, A. C., & Jamieson, S. (2018). Ethical dilemmas and reflexivity in qualitative research. *Perspectives on Medical Education*, *7*(2), 69–75.

Rivero, C., Du Toit, P., & Kotze, H. (2003). Tracking the development of the middle class in democratic South Africa. *Politeia*, *22*(3), 6–29.

Roberts, B., Struwig, J., Gordon, S., Viljoen, J., & Wentzel, M. (2012). Financial literacy in South Africa: Results of a baseline national survey. Pretoria: Financial Services Board.

Ryan, C. (2018). Claims of discrimination against black FNB customers heads to court. The Citizen. 4.12.2018, Retrieved from https://citizen.co.za/business/2045100/claims-of-discrimination-against-black-fnb-customers-heads-to-court/

Sarkisian, N., & Gerstel, N. (2006). Marriage: The good, the bad, and the greedy. *Contexts*, *5*(4), 16–21.

Seekings, J., & Nattrass, N. (2006). *Class, race and inequality in South Africa*. Durban, South Africa: UKZN Press.

Seekings, J. (2009). The rise and fall of the Weberian analysis of class in South Africa between 1949 and the early 1970s. *Journal of Southern African Studies*, *35*(4), 865–881.

Seekings, J. (2010). The rise and fall of the Weberian analysis of class in South Africa between 1949 and the early 1970s. *Journal of Southern African Studies, 35*(4), 865–881.

Seekings, J. (2013). *Welfare regimes and distribution across the global South: Theory and evidence in the construction of typologies*. Unpublished paper.

Simbürger, E. (2014). Reflexivity in qualitative social research: Bridging the gap between theory and practice with Alvin Gouldner's reflexive sociology. *Magis, Revista Internacional de Investigación en Educación, 7*(14), 55–68.

Smith, T. D. (2008). *Decolonizing methodologies: Research and indigenous peoples*. London: Zed Books.

Southall, R. (2013). Political change and the black middle class in democratic South Africa. Retrieved form http://ccs.ukzn.ac.za/copyright.html

Southall, R. (2016). *The new black middle class in South Africa*. Auckland Park, South Africa: Jacana.

Spronk, R. (2016). *The making of the middle classes: From Kula Raha to sophistication in Nairobi*. Geneva: Kompreno.

St. Drake, C., & Clayton, H. R. (1945). *Black metropolis: A study of Negro life in a northern city*. New York, NY: Brace and Company.

Statistics South Africa. (2009). Retrived from www.statssa.gov.za

Sutter, M., Bosman, R., Kocher, M. G., & van Winden, F. 2009. Gender pairing and bargaining—beware the same sex! *Experimental Economics, 12*(3), 318–331.

Van Fleet, D. D., & Atwater, L. (1997). Gender neutral names: Do not be so sure! *Sex Role: A Journal of Research, 37*(1–2): 111–123.

Veblen, T. (1899). *The theory of the leisure class*. New York, NY: Macmillan.

Visagie, J. (2011). *The development of the middle class in post-apartheid South Africa*. Retrieved form http://www.aceconferences.co.za/MASA%20FULL%20PAPERS/Visagie,%20J.pdf

Visagie, J. (2013). 'Race, gender and growth of the affluent middle class in post-apartheid South Africa'. *Biennial conference of the economic society of South Africa.* University of the Free State, Bloemfontein, South Africa.

Wilson, W. J. (1978). *The declining significance of race: Blacks and changing American institutions*. Chicago, IL: University of Chicago Press.

Zoch, A. (2015). Life Chance and class: Estimating inequality of opportunity for children and adolescents in South Africa. *Development Southern Africa*, 32 (1), 57–75.

INDEX

Note: Page numbers followed by "*n*" with numbers indicate notes.

Accoutrements, 49
Advanced degrees, 29, 59
Affirmative action, 107
African Development Bank, 1
African(s), 4–5, 34*n*3, 36, 89
names, 89
Age, 13, 18, 20, 27–28, 31, 44, 49, 86, 105, 114, 116, 145
Agency, 12, 127
American privilege, 80, 132
Apartheid, 2, 3, 5–7, 9–10, 36, 38, 41–42, 48, 61, 66, 70, 73, 108, 117, 119, 125, 139, 143
Appearing casual, 123
Assumption(s), 11, 16, 19–20, 46, 48–49, 70, 72, 84, 89, 103–104, 108, 114–116, 123, 126, 130, 136, 146

Belief, 12, 19, 55, 77–78, 114, 146
Black academics, 26
Black American woman, 24, 26
Black bourgeoisie, 73, 78–79, 146
Black church, 119
Black diamonds, 107
Black girl magic, 107
Black identity, 70, 75
Black middle class (BMC), 1–2, 7–11, 14, 17–19, 25–26, 28, 35–63, 65–70, 72–73, 75–80, 85, 87, 94, 106, 110, 113, 119, 123, 125–127, 129–132, 136–137, 139, 143–144, 146
Black solidarity, 75
Black South African, 26, 31, 44, 68, 143

Black-African, 30
Blackness, 9–10, 36, 42, 65, 68, 70, 72–74, 83, 116, 140
Blue-collar professions, 8
Body language, 20, 97, 99, 114
Bottom-up approach, 107

Car ownership, 55
Catching gender, 18, 87
Church clothes, 117
Citizenship, 1, 18, 86, 145–146
Class
   analysis, 17, 86
   position, 5, 13, 17–18, 40–41, 43, 61, 70, 75, 85, 87, 105, 120, 127, 141
   status, 8, 13, 31–32, 54, 57, 65, 67
   stratification, 19, 76, 113
Clever Blacks, 65–82
Clothing, 115, 118–119, 122, 136
Coloured participants, 30, 34n3, 36
Comfort zone, 96
Community mobilisation, 35
Conception(s), 8, 10–11, 18, 36–37, 39–42, 46, 50, 54, 70, 76, 87, 116
Conceptual tap-dance, 57
Conceptualizing the Black middle class, 22

Conspicuous consumption, 9–11, 44, 49–50, 54, 79, 83
Consumption patterns, 35
Contact hypothesis, 77
Contested concept, 12–14, 69, 84
Contextual information, 96
Converse sneakers, 116
Counter identities, 87
Creative reflexivity, 145
Credit, 38
   access, 48, 51
   scores, 46, 47
Critical analysis, 16
Critical reflection, 15, 55
Critical reflexivity, 15
Cross-national class, 8
Cross-racial class, 8
Cultural capital, 51, 62, 68
Cultural crossings, 70
Cultural differences, 92, 101, 136
Cultural system, 17, 86

Data, 13–14, 31–32, 88, 100, 134
   collection process, 24, 46, 49, 123, 126–127, 144
Debt, 10, 45–52, 64
Demographic group, 32–33, 40–41, 69, 81, 146
Detachment, 90
Discrimination, 2, 5, 19, 41, 45, 48, 66, 113, 121, 143–144
Diversity, 12, 82

Domestic chores, 107
Dress, 19–20, 61, 113–124, 141, 146
 consciousness, 123

Economic capital, 68–69
Emancipation, 75
Embodied experience, 115
Empirical value, 42
Empowering, 108
Ethics clearance, 30
Ethnicity, 18, 48, 86, 146
Evolving definition(s), 37, 42, 48–49
Expensive clothes, 54, 117
Experience gap, 68
Eye contact, 91–92, 94
Eyeing me out, 101

Fact of Blackness, 36
Fashion, 115–116, 123
Feminist scholars, 17, 85–86
Fieldwork, 17, 22–23, 31, 37, 40, 46, 52, 63, 86, 94, 100, 106, 122, 143
Financial education, 47–48
Financial literacy, 46–49
Financial management, 46, 48–50
Financial stability, 52
First impressions matter, 115
Fixed position, 16
Food, 33, 39, 59, 105, 114–115, 122, 124–130, 136, 141, 146

Food accepting, 19, 128–129
Formal dress, 122
Fragility of Black middle class, 12, 145
Fulbright fellowship, 22, 132

Gauteng, South Africa, 25, 30
Gender, 13, 16–21, 48, 86–87, 89–90, 96, 100–111, 121, 145
 analysis, 17–18, 85
 Gender matching, 88–96, 104
 neutral, 89, 120
 norms, 17, 86
 script, 111
 gender-sensitive research, 91
Gendering, 87–88, 95, 100, 103
Good Blacks, 73
Good manners, 119, 124–125

Hair, 75
Health, 35
Heterogeneous nature of research team, 26
Highly privileged" members, 57, 81
Historical analysis, 4, 36
Historical capital, 70
Home improvements, 29, 41, 54–55, 93, 98, 116, 122, 125, 129

Home ownership, 9, 54
Homogenised construction, 10

In-depth interviews, 88
Indebtedness, 48, 83
Indians, 34*n*3, 36
Inequalities, 2, 34*n*3, 52
Inequities, 8–9, 45
Insider/outsider standpoint, 26
Insiderness, 14, 16, 67–68, 75, 132
Insiders, 2, 14–15, 24, 68
Institutional Review Board (IRB), 22
Inter-disciplinary scholarship, 36
Interest rates, 48
Intergenerational wealth, 48
Internal conflict, 78
Interpretive information, 96
Interview process, 13–15, 19–20, 26, 32, 59, 65, 81, 84, 90–91, 96–102, 104, 113–115, 127, 145–146
Interviewees, 13, 95, 108
Interviewers, 13, 15, 88–89
Intimate relationships, 25
Issues of affordability, 17, 85
Iterative processes, 144

Johannesburg, South Africa, 22, 30, 138

Language, 5, 10, 13, 75–76, 119, 136–137, 139
Lazy, 106–108
Lesbian and bisexual Black women, 25
Living beyond their means, 10

Macro level's of people's lives, 17, 86
Marginalisation, 18, 45, 86, 144
Marital status, 13, 28
Markers of middle classness, 31, 54
Market research, 54
Marriage, 35
Marx, Karl, 57
Masculinities, 25, 91, 116
Mate selection, 35
Material goods, 44, 63
Matrix, 12, 56
Meaning making, 18, 86
Melrose arch, 130, 135, 138–140
Methodology, 19–20, 32, 114–115
Micro level, 17, 86
Microcosm, 141
Middle class generosity, 124–130
Middle classness, 8, 11, 17–23, 31, 33, 36, 40, 51, 53–57, 59, 61, 68–70, 72–73, 77, 86–87, 113–140
Middle class Blacks, 9
Mortgage loans, 48
Moving target, 35–63

Neighbourhood location, 9
Nigerian, 24–25, 67–68

Non-compliance, 117
Normative narrative, 41

Objective indicators, 7
Oppressive discourses, 95
Oppressive middle class, 7
Outsiderness, 14, 16, 75
Outsiders, 2, 14–15, 24, 68
Overdressed, 121
Oxymoron, 49

Participants, 2, 30, 51–53, 60–61, 81, 87–91, 95–96, 98–106, 115–118, 120, 122–128, 130, 132, 134–135, 145–146
Participation in the arts, 35
Patriarchy, 105
Pay their own way, 105
Perception, 19–20, 26, 32, 67–82, 114–115, 117, 121–122, 124–125, 136, 144, 146
Performance of middle class, 33, 141
Performance tool, 120
Performativity, 116
Personal development, 131
Personal experiences, 13, 16, 32, 104
Personal narratives, 21, 33
PhD, 61, 68
Physical appearance, 19, 113–114, 146
Physical mobilities, 70
Pick n pay, 134
Pilot interviews, 22, 30

Political activism, 35
Politics of representation, 18
Politics of respectability, 119
Positionality, 10, 12, 15–16, 23, 26, 32, 67–68
Post-fieldwork meetings, 40
Power differentials, 85
Power dynamics, 88, 95, 101–102
Precarious position, 17, 70, 86
Preconceived ideas, 15–16, 20, 46, 65–66, 82–84, 115, 122, 136, 145
Prejudice, 2, 19, 66, 77, 113
Pretentious, 67
Principal investigators, 23–26
Privilege, 5, 18, 25, 39, 63, 80, 86, 125, 139, 146
Props, 20, 114
Public discourse, 71, 95, 106–107

Qualitative research, 15, 24

Race, 2, 5–7, 12–13, 19–20, 22–23, 26, 33, 35, 43–45, 48, 50, 57–58, 68, 73–74, 76, 113–114, 129, 143
Racial disparities, 8, 10
Racial identity, 26, 41, 72, 75–76
Racial identity in white spaces, 26
Racial segregation, 5, 143

Real black, the, 73
Reconstruction, 106
Reflective process, 15, 66
Reflexivity, 2, 12–18, 33, 77, 83, 86–87, 95, 145
Region, 19, 113
Research
  enterprise, 13, 32
  participants, 14–16, 20, 83–84, 95–96, 115
Researcher
  bias, 15, 24
  subjectivity, 144
  voice, 20, 32–33, 146
  worldview, 15
Resistance, 126, 127
Respectability, 118–119
  politics, 119

Safety of participant, 98
Sandton, 105, 130
Security check, 97–98
Segregation, 5, 45, 66, 144
Self-growth, 61
Self-identification, 10–11, 30–31, 38, 64, 144
Self-monitoring, 15
Self-sufficiency, 127
Sexual advances, 101
Sexual gestures, 124–125
Sexuality, 13
Sexualisation, 100–102
Social
  buffer, 41
  capital, 68, 139
  experiences, 18, 86
  integration, 66
  location, 14, 17, 85, 135
  markers, 90
  mobility, 2, 45, 66, 70, 80, 144
  movements, 35
  power physical appearance, 114
  progress, 54
  strata, 135
  stratification, 19, 113
  systems, 17, 86
  taboo, 116
Socio-economic, 8, 13, 16, 18, 24, 32, 36, 49, 52, 57, 66, 86, 120, 144, 146
  status, 146
  well-being, 7
Soweto, Johannesburg, 24–25
Static positions, 14
Stereotypes, 104–111
Stratified societies, 85, 118
Streetwise, 116–117
Stuck-up, 67
Subjectivities, 15–16, 91
Subthemes, 37–38
Suburbs, 9, 54, 72, 138
Sunday best clothes, 119

Themes, 21
Theoretical value, 42–43
Theorising, 2, 13, 15, 41, 144
Township, 3, 6–7, 9, 54, 72, 109–110, 115–116
Traditional gender role, 99, 107

Uber, 71, 128
Unemployment, 17, 85
Unequal ownership of banks, 51
University of Johannesburg, 22–23, 30, 34n2
University of Maryland, 20–21
University of Witwatersrand, 22, 24
Upper classes, 118

Wealth accumulation, 10, 35
Wealth expenditure, 10
Weber, Max, 57

Well-being, 7, 21, 35
Well-off black, 70, 75
White collar, 8
White supremacy, 42
Whiteness, 10, 42, 116–117
Working class, 6, 10, 25, 41, 69–70, 74, 106–107, 117, 119, 123, 127–128

Young Black woman, 106–110

Zulu, 92, 138
Zuma, Jacob, 74